PATRICK HENRY,
PROPHET OF THE REVOLUTION

PATRICK HENRY, by Thomas Sully, after a miniature painted about 1792.
Courtesy of The Colonial Williamsburg Foundation.

PATRICK HENRY,
PROPHET OF THE REVOLUTION

By Jane Carson

Edward M. Riley, *Editor*

Published by the

Virginia Independence Bicentennial Commission

Box JF

Williamsburg, Virginia 23185

I.

The Homer of Orators

THE compelling eloquence of Patrick Henry was already legendary in his lifetime. Years after his death people who had heard him speak still remembered vividly how they felt under his spell, and accounts of his most famous orations became apocryphal.

When his first biographer, William Wirt, discovered in 1805 that the text of none of Henry's great revolutionary speeches had ever existed, he collected the reminiscences of old men who had known the orator intimately. Eager to preserve the memory of Henry as an inspiration for young men, Wirt followed the classical conventions of his day; using Livy's sketches of the great Romans as a model, he made his biography a textbook on rhetoric, patriotism, and morality. Himself a talented speaker, he put together the collected bits and pieces with such skill that his reconstructions of the Caesar-Brutus speech and the Liberty-or-Death speech have become the best-known American examples of spell-binding oratory, favorite declamations of schoolboys displaying their talents to admiring parents on visitors' day.

Henry usually spoke extemporaneously, from rough notes; he did not write out his speeches ahead of time because he did not know how far he should go with his argument until he could test his audience reaction. He was a persuasive speaker for this very reason. There were no newspaper reporters then to take down his words as he spoke them; in the House of Burgesses and the revolutionary conventions he usually spoke in the Committee of the Whole, and the clerk made no notes for the official journals.

While there is still some doubt about what Henry really said on each occasion and what Wirt invented, there is no doubt at all about his effect. All his contemporaries—friends and opponents alike—

testified to the tremendous power of his eloquence even when they could not remember exactly what he said or describe in detail just how he said it. This ability to engage the sympathies of an audience and move it to action has always been the measure of oratorical power. Demosthenes, Cicero, Shakespeare's Mark Anthony and King Henry V, Addison's Cato; the evangelists George Whitefield and Samuel Davies—all these orators, well known to colonial Virginians, had this mysterious ability, hard to analyze but instantly recognized in the emotional response to its magic.

When George Mason first heard Henry speak, he decided: "Every word he says not only engages but commands the attention; and your passions are no longer your own when he addresses them."

His son-in-law, Judge Spencer Roane, explained: "The tones of his voice, to say nothing of his manner and gestures, were insinuated into the feelings of his hearers in a manner that baffled all description. It seemed to operate by mere sympathy, and by his tones alone it seemed to me that he could make you cry or laugh at pleasure."

The custodian of Carpenters' Hall, hearing him speak in Philadelphia, thought his dramatic effect was cumulative. He rose slowly, with an air of diffidence, and began to speak hesitantly. Then, "as he warmed to his subject, his cheeks glowed, his eyes flashed, and his voice, rich and strong, rang through and filled the hall."

Edmund Randolph believed that no one could doubt Henry's sincerity, that "he transferred into the breasts of others the earnestness depicted in his own features." He used no oratorical tricks or "unmeaning expletives for effect." His voice was "melodious, diversified by a mixture of sensations which a dramatic versatility of action and of countenance produced." He was a master of the effective pause; yet "his eye never strayed about in quest of applause." He was often humorous but never frivolous; "arguments which at first seemed strange" were afterwards found to be "select in their kind, because adapted to some peculiarity of his audience." His imagination "painted to the soul" and "eclipsed the sparklings of art." His most effective figures of speech came from the Bible or "the sublime scenes and objects of nature"; his own "lightning consisted in quick successive flashes," and "for grand impressions in the defense of liberty, the Western world has not yet been able to exhibit a rival."

When Jefferson said that Henry spoke "as Homer wrote," his contemporaries knew precisely what he meant. The well-educated had read *The Odyssey* and *The Iliad* in Greek; others knew the stories as they knew the Bible and Shakespeare, from reading them in English or from hearing them. Like Homer's Greeks, they lived in the country or in small towns and took pleasure in the sights and sounds of everyday things in nature. Everyone knew that Homer's plots and characters, his proverbs and pithy sayings, were traditional, that he made them his own by giving them different twists in new combinations or settings. Henry made similar use of familiar sayings from the Bible, Shakespeare, mythology, historical characters and events; with superb timing and a new twist, a familiar quotation or analogy would catch the attention of an audience and hold it. The electric effect of his "Liberty or Death," for example, received an extra charge in the ear that recognized Cato's words in Addison's play:

"The hand of fate is over us, and heav'n
Exacts severity from all our thoughts:
It is not now a time to talk of ought
But chains, or conquest; liberty, or death."

The musical cadence of Homer's poetry was the classic hexameter. In Henry's prose one heard the cadences of the King James version of the Bible. Like Homer's, Henry's words came from the ordinary speech of the common man. Randolph noticed his "homespun pronunciation" and found his "language sometimes peculiar, and even quaint," while at the same time it was "expressive and appropriate." He used the natural words for things, without the "poetic embellishment" of artificial or bookish phrases so popular with nineteenth-century translators of Homer and biographers of Henry, all trying to "improve" their subjects. Henry was a plain man who preferred a plain style of living, plain clothing, a plain diet, and plain words.

II.

From Obscurity to Notoriety, 1736-1765

PATRICK HENRY was born May 29, 1736, in lower Hanover County
about eight miles from the site of Richmond, at Studley, where his
mother lived as wife and widow of Col. John Syme and then as wife of
John Henry. Studley was a prosperous farm with open fields,
woodlands, and a small meandering stream, Totopotomoy Creek.
The comfortable house of two stories was surrounded by
outbuildings—storage and working facilities for housekeeping, sta-
ble, barn, and pens for domestic animals. The nearby county seat,
Hanover Courthouse, was scarcely a village, and the nearest town,
Newcastle on the Pamunkey River, was five miles away.

In this interesting playground for a little boy, Patrick spent his
childhood with two elder brothers, six younger sisters, numerous
cousins and neighbors. Through his mother's parents he was kin to a
large family of Winstons and Dabneys who came to Virginia in the
seventeenth century and now belonged to the Hanover gentry. His
father had come to Hanover from Scotland about ten years before
Patrick's birth; with mathematical training at King's College, Aber-
deen, he was prepared to be a surveyor, and he speculated in frontier
lands in upper Hanover, Goochland, and Albemarle counties. Like
his wife's relatives, John Henry was appointed to local office. In 1737
he was a Hanover justice, a vestryman, and a major in the county
militia; ten years later he was Colonel Henry. His brother, the
Reverend Patrick Henry, who had followed him to Virginia, became a
neighbor in 1737 as rector of St. Paul's Parish—in good time to help
with the education of young Patrick, his namesake.

The nature and quality of his schooling are not definitely known. A
brother-in-law, Col. Samuel Meredith, and a son-in-law, Judge
Spencer Roane, agreed that he studied the three R's in a neighbor-

4

hood school until he was ten, then spent five years under his father's tutelage. Colonel Henry was a good teacher, who later opened a private school with a dozen students and enlarged it to accommodate twenty boys. Patrick's favorite subjects were ancient and modern history, mathematics, geography, and natural philosophy (science). Scholarship never had the appeal to him that it held for his father and uncle and for his friend Thomas Jefferson; yet he mastered history and the classics well enough to quote them freely all his life, and in correct Latin when it was suitable. (He told John Adams that he had read Virgil and Livy when he was a boy.)

He learned to enjoy reading things that interested him, to think about what he read and test it against his own observation; thus books contributed a variety of practical ideas to his thinking, and he had a phenomenal memory. Though he always belittled his formal education, he passed the eighteenth-century test of an educated gentleman: he could put a sentence together with precision and force.

From his parents and uncle he received the conventional training in religion and morals, with especially thorough grounding in the Bible and the Anglican catechism. When he was an old man, he quoted for a grandson the series of moral principles instilled by his Uncle Patrick: "To be true and just in all my dealings. To bear no malice nor hatred in my heart. To keep my hands from picking and stealing. Not to covet other men's goods; but to learn and labor truly to get my own living, and to do my duty in that state of life unto which it shall please God to call me."

When Patrick was about fourteen years old, the family moved to his father's piedmont farm twenty miles to the west. The Mount Brilliant house was new, and the farm had fewer cultivated fields, with rolling hills and woodlands stretching down to the South Anna River. This kind of environment appealed to him, and all his life his own homes fit the pattern.

Tobacco farming was not to his taste, and at the age of fifteen he went to work in a country store, first as clerk, then as partner of his brother William. The Henry brothers, Hanover merchants, went out of business within the year. While he was closing out the store accounts, the eighteen-year-old Patrick married a neighbor's daughter, Sarah Shelton, aged sixteen. It was probably a love match, for in eighteenth-century custom, parents arranged marriages when large amounts of property were involved. Colonel Henry was in financial difficulties at the time, but John Shelton gave them three hundred acres of land, a tract called Pine Slash, with six slaves to work it. Here the young couple set up housekeeping, and Patrick was a tobacco farmer for three years—until an accidental fire destroyed their dwelling house and all the furnishings. They lived in an overseer's cabin for a time, while Patrick continued to farm his lands and opened another country store with capital raised by the sale of some of his slaves. Within two years he was broke again, chiefly because he was unable to collect the debts carried on his books.

At this point, in 1759, he decided to become a lawyer, a sensible decision because most people employed lawyers to collect bad debts, and there was plenty of that kind of law business, as he well knew. He closed the store and went to live with his father-in-law in the tavern at Hanover Courthouse while he studied for the bar examination.

These embarrassing circumstances did not affect his optimistic disposition or dampen his enthusiasm for the pleasant social life of the community. At a Christmas party in the home of Col. Nathaniel West Dandridge he met Thomas Jefferson, who remembered the holidays as a time when he saw Henry almost every day at some festivity in the neighborhood, and the two young men became good friends. Though the young Jefferson was a serious person who usually valued conversation for the information it supplied his inquiring mind, he responded to Henry's relaxed warmth and sociability. Trying to analyze the famous Henry popularity, Jefferson pointed to excellence in fiddling, dancing, and the kind of "pleasantry" which "attached everyone to him." Knowing the story of the recent business calamities, Jefferson was surprised to see that "his misfortunes were not to be traced, either in his countenance or conduct."

Spring of 1760 found him ready to take the bar examination. The extent and method of his preparation are unknown. It was customary then to prepare for the bar as an apprentice in another lawyer's office, studying law books, doing independent reading and legal research, drafting legal papers under the direction of a practicing attorney. Most Virginia lawyers who made a living from their profession followed this routine: George Wythe, Edmund Pendleton, Thomas Jefferson, John Marshall, for example. An exceptional few, like Sir John Randolph and his sons Peyton and John, studied law in London at the Inns of Court as part of a gentleman's education, but they too trained for active practice in the Virginia courts by practical work with Virginia lawyers. In colonial courts the judges were laymen, more interested in practical justice than in technical niceties of the law. The more flexible a lawyer's style and the broader his experience, the better. He won his case by convincing judges and jury that his client was in the right according to their standards of justice and not by citing obscure legal precedents which laymen might not recognize and understand.

Henry departed from the established pattern and studied alone. Col. Peter Fontaine gave him a volume of forms for declarations and pleas. He borrowed law books, including the standard "Coke on Littleton," the Virginia *Statutes at Large,* and probably Matthew Bacon's *Abridgement of the Laws.* (Bacon's handbook became famous in Tennessee when Andrew Jackson cited it so often that the opposing counsel gave him a slab of smoked pork; the joke did not amuse the young solicitor, who wrote out a challenge to a duel on the fly-leaf of his copy of Bacon. Henry would use a similar blank page to jot down his Stamp Act Resolves.) In a short time, variously estimated between six months and six weeks, he learned how to write out legal forms, to follow prescribed procedures in court, to find precedents in Virginia and English laws which would support the positions of his clients.

Virginia law required that candidates for a license to practice in the colony go to Williamsburg and apply to a panel of examiners appointed by the General Court. As many of this panel as were in town then questioned the candidate separately and passed judgment on his "capacity, ability and fitness." Henry was examined by Robert Carter Nicholas, George Wythe, Peyton and John Randolph. Shocked by his careless dress and country manners, the learned gentlemen soon found him well informed in general history, adequate in the common law, and deficient in municipal law; yet they liked the way his mind worked, and John Randolph and Wythe signed his license with the understanding that he would continue his studies.

While he was in Williamsburg he called on Jefferson at the College of William and Mary, but he had no other friends in the capital and did not comment on his impressions of the largest town he had ever seen, the place where every ambitious lawyer hoped to practice before the General Court or perhaps one day sit in the House of Burgesses.

Back home with his license, he immediately began to practice in Hanover and Goochland counties. His first clients were relatives and neighbors for whom he handled the routine business of drawing wills and administering estates, and he pled cases involving debts, land

7

claims, slander and other personal disputes. His fee books show that in the first eight months of practice he handled 176 cases for about seventy clients and collected more than half of his fees, sometimes in small cash payments of ten shillings or less, sometimes in produce and other goods.

In three years he handled 1185 cases for a growing number of clients who now included prominent planters, Scottish merchants and their factors, land speculators and other businessmen as far away as the frontier. During these years he qualified for practice in the courts of Cumberland, Louisa, Albemarle, Chesterfield, and Augusta counties and often traveled long distances on horseback. Most of his cases were still petty, but he was making a good living from the large volume of his practice, and his reputation as a hard-working, conscientious attorney who could win cases for his clients was growing with his successful practice.

Suddenly at the end of 1763 Patrick Henry's name could be heard in every Virginia parish, where "the Parsons' Cause" was a cause célèbre. Today the whole affair seems trivial, his participation in it was accidental, and his fee was only fifteen shillings; yet it was important to him because it was his first opportunity to appeal to a wide audience.

The salary of each Anglican minister was paid by his parish, sixteen thousand pounds of tobacco from the parish levy, which was collected in tobacco. It was an inconvenient way to be paid, and the value of the salary was uncertain. But this uncertainty was shared by all Virginians because the economy was governed by the price of tobacco on the world market. Many clergymen of course preferred a set salary in pounds sterling. When the General Assembly passed an act permitting payment in money, the rate was set at two pence per pound, an average rate rather than the current one, when the market price of tobacco was higher. The clergy, organized in protest, went over the head of the Virginia legislature and appealed to the king to disallow the Two-penny Acts of 1755 and 1758. This was done, and individual clergymen then brought suit for damages.

The third suit in the series was tried in Hanover, where the plaintiff, the Rev. James Maury, was represented by Peter Lyons, the king's attorney. John Lewis, an experienced lawyer, represented the defendants, the tax collectors. In November of 1763 the court decided in favor of the plaintiff, and a jury was summoned to meet a month later and decide the amount of the damages Maury should receive.

Lewis felt that he had lost the case and retired. For his last-minute substitute, Patrick Henry, there was nothing left to do except persuade the jury to vote token damages, and the best way to accomplish that was by an appeal to their prejudices. Maury complained that Henry "harangued the jury for near an hour" and ranged widely from the case at hand. The lawyer knew many of the jurors personally. Some of them were dissenters, who had to pay parish levies for Anglican clergymen and then privately support their own ministers from additional funds. Therefore, he inveighed against an established church, against individual clergymen who neglected parish duties, whose greed for money led them to flout the law made by their neighbors and a "benevolent" Governor and Council and persuade distant London officials to disallow the good Virginia law. He cited a basic constitutional principle in English law, that only a representative legislature should set taxes for the people who paid them—an idea later argued as "no taxation without representation." This was treason, perhaps, but the bench did not interrupt him, possibly because his father was the presiding judge. The jury responded to the "harangue" by voting one penny to Maury.

Henry's constitutional argument was not original or startlingly new in colonial political thought. John Locke had popularized it in England nearly a hundred years earlier, and it was already being developed for colonial application, notably in Richard Bland's *A Letter to the Clergy of Virginia* (1760). But Henry first argued it in public to a group of ordinary citizens, and he spoke with such persuasive force that his fame spread throughout the colony.

Where he learned how to talk so effectively no one knows precisely. Edmund Randolph thought that he always knew instinctively "what chord of the heart would sound in unison with his immediate purpose, and with what strength or peculiarity it ought to be touched." If he was born with a special talent for reading minds and hearts, he developed it into an art by close observation and long practice. He understood people because he was sincerely interested in them, approachable and warmly sympathetic. He was pleasant and cheerful with everyone, Judge Roane said, and had "a remarkable faculty of adapting himself to his company" because he found something in common with everyone he met and felt at home everywhere he went.

His "great delight was in coversation, and in the society of his friends and family." Conversation to him was an exchange of ideas; he was a good listener and could ask leading questions that would draw out other people and enliven the exchange. His own remarks were more likely to be imaginative or humorous than didactic or informative, and he had a large repertoire of anecdotes which he told with great skill. When he became a lawyer at the age of twenty-four, he was already widely experienced in private conversation and needed only to adapt his skills in more public talk to larger groups of the kinds of people he had known all his life. He could catch a jury's attention and entertain them or make them laugh or arouse their sympathy for his client and persuade them to vote in his favor.

The following year another case took him to Williamsburg. It concerned a contested election in Hanover. His client was his friend Col. Nathaniel West Dandridge, Jefferson's host at the Christmas party. Dandridge charged that his successful opponent, James Littlepage, had won his seat in the House of Burgesses through "undue" influence if not bribery. Henry appeared before the House Committee of Privileges and Elections and presented his client's argument. The members of this prestigious committee included the most influential burgesses, polished gentlemen-scholars quite different from Hanover justices and jurymen. They thought the young lawyer seemed ill at ease, awkward, and carelessly dressed. He probably was uncomfortable in this group of impressive strangers and painfully conscious of the weaknesses in his client's case. When he began to speak and ranged off into a moving oration on the sacredness of the suffrage, the gentlemen gave him their full attention and admired his eloquence, but they were not completely carried away. They decided that Littlepage had won the election honestly, and he took his seat in the House of Burgesses.

At the next session of the General Assembly, in the spring of 1765, Henry appeared as the new burgess from Louisa County, where he owned a farm and was therefore eligible for election. The new house under construction on a hill overlooking Roundabout Valley would be his home as soon as it was finished. His growing legal practice and local reputation were providing stepping stones toward financial security and political prominence.

The burgesses now included statesmen who rank as high in talent for government as any group ever assembled in the western world—Virginia's proudest contribution to history. Speaker John Robinson for twenty-five years presided over the house and was also treasurer of the colony, a landed aristocrat with great prestige and power. Peyton Randolph, son of Sir John, educated at the Middle

Temple, attorney general since 1744, was a dignified, affable man whose opinion in constitutional matters was highly regarded. Richard Bland, kinsman of the Randolphs, was "one of the oldest, ablest and most respected members," a skilled parliamentarian and political philosopher who would become the chief pamphleteer for the cause of Virginia liberties. George Wythe, the most learned jurist in the colonies, was noted for his pure patriotism, integrity, and personal charm. He was a classical scholar and a great teacher; Jefferson and Marshall would be two of his students. George Washington, a well-to-do planter at Mount Vernon, was valued for his strength of character and sound common sense and respected for his military record as commander-in-chief of the Virginia forces in the French and Indian War. Robert Carter Nicholas, the most successful lawyer in the colony, lived in Williamsburg and belonged to the tidewater gentry. Edmund Pendleton, the most skillful trial lawyer in Virginia, was equally effective in political argument; Jefferson thought him "the ablest man in debate" he ever encountered but "the kindest friend, the most amiable and pleasant of companions." Like Henry, Pendleton came from the up-country but as a protégé of Speaker Robinson, Pendleton voted with "the old guard." Richard Henry Lee was a polished orator, especially effective in small groups of leaders. With his brother Francis Lightfoot Lee he had been a burgess since 1758, representing the landed gentry of the Northern Neck but ready to work with Henry and Jefferson and other young leaders of the revolutionary movement.

Patrick Henry—a new member of this distinguished assembly, ignorant of parliamentary procedure, young, with no connections or prestige—was expected to sit quietly and learn from more experienced statesmen. But he deliberately challenged the old leadership. First, he opposed Speaker Robinson on a bill to establish a public loan office for the use of planters suffering from a prolonged depression in the tobacco market. Henry opposed the bill on principle, as an example of favoritism: it would pay the debts of a few individual planters at public expense. He did not know the real purpose of the bill because it was a closely guarded secret. The Speaker, as Treasurer of Virginia, had already lent public money to friends in a total amount of £100,000, and this bill was to enable him to float these secret private loans with public money, openly. The political effect of Henry's opposition was to establish him as a bold spokesman for up-country farmers against the vested interests of the great tidewater planters who controlled the political life of the colony.

His challenge to the old leaders became perfectly clear on May 29, when a new item of business came up for discussion—the Stamp Act just passed by the Parliament of Great Britain. The Seven Years War, though gloriously successful, had been expensive, and English businessmen were complaining about the high taxes required to pay for it and to administer the enormous new territory won from France. On the principle that the American colonies should help to pay for the North American part of the expenses, the Grenville ministry placed an excise tax on newspapers and a variety of legal papers. As with playing cards and cigarettes today, stamps had to be attached to the specified articles before they could be sold or used. While the stamps were inexpensive, they had to be paid for in cash, which was scarce in the colonies, where credit economies were the rule. And while the use of the stamps was a nuisance to nearly everyone, the businessmen especially affected were lawyers and newspaper men, the professional propagandists of the day. Understandably, criticisms of the proposed new tax were immediate and widespread.

During the year 1764, when the plan was being discussed, the General Assembly had expressed the colony's opposition to it in a series of formal petitions addressed to the king, the House of Lords, and the House of Commons, stating their objections in clear, precise language. This was the recognized constitutional procedure. But the Virginia petitions, like those from the other colonies, were ignored, and the Stamp Act became law in January, to go into effect in November. Now, in May, the only proper procedure was to negotiate for its repeal, preferably with the collaboration of other British American colonies. To refuse to obey it would be sedition; to reject it alone would be suicide.

As soon as the question was introduced, Henry took the floor from the burgesses who had prepared the earlier petitions and presented a series of resolutions restating the objections in more forceful language. His theme was this: By royal charter King James guaranteed to Virginians all the rights and privileges of Englishmen at home, and none of these rights had been forfeited "or in any other way given up." Rather, they had been "constantly recognized by the Kings and People of Great Britain." The stamp tax levied by Parliament—not by the General Assembly—was an example of taxation without representation, a violation of the sacred heritage of all freeborn Englishmen.

The resolutions were opposed by Randolph, Robinson, Nicholas,

Bland, and Wythe, who argued that they made no new statement of the colony's position, and repetition at this time was useless as well as redundant. Several burgesses from new counties beyond the tidewater—John Fleming of Cumberland, George Johnston of Fairfax, Robert Munford of Mecklenburg, Paul Carrington of Charlotte—supported the resolutions. Pendleton had already left town, along with other burgesses who thought the main business of the session was finished. The "thin" house of thirty-nine members debated the resolutions for the greater part of two days and passed five of them in amended form. The afternoon of May 30 Henry, too, left town, pleased with his performance as a "freshman burgess" who had successfully challenged "the old guard" for leadership in the House of Burgesses. But he was quite unaware of what its cumulative effect would be when exaggerated reports reached the other colonies.

The next day, May 31, his more conservative opponents had a majority in the house, and they voted to expunge the fifth resolution from the official journal because they considered it "inflammatory." We do not know precisely what it was. Neither Henry nor his supporters kept a copy of all the resolutions as he proposed them. The *Virginia Gazette* did not print them in any form because the conservative editor, Joseph Royle, was also the public printer and did not wish to offend the establishment.

Somehow newspapers in other colonies obtained copies which differed considerably from the official version in the Journal of the House of Burgesses. The *Newport Mercury* printed six resolutions on June 24; the *Boston Gazette* printed a preamble and seven resolves on July 1; the *Maryland Gazette* on July 4 published seven resolves without a preamble. Other newspapers throughout the colonies picked up the story and issued it without citing a Virginia source, and we shall never know where the accounts came from. Did the supporters of the resolves quickly send them off to friends outside Virginia, as they were originally planned, before they were amended and rearranged during the two-day debate? Probably. Governor Francis Fauquier informed the British government that there were seven resolves in all, but their advocates kept the last two in their pockets after "the difficulty they had in carrying the 5th which was by a single voice, and knowing them to be more virulent and inflammatory." In all the newspaper versions the last two resolves advocated resistance:

> *Resolved,* That his Majesty's liege People, the Inhabitants
> of this Colony, are not bound to yield Obedience to any Law

or Ordinance whatsoever, designed to impose any Taxation whatsoever upon them, other than the Laws or Ordinances of the General Assembly aforesaid.

Resolved, That any Person, who shall, by speaking or writing, assert or maintain, that any Person or Persons, other than the General Assembly of this Colony, have any Right or Authority to impose or lay any Taxation on the People here, shall be deemed an Enemy of this his Majesty's Colony.

Only one eye-witness account of the debate was written down when it occurred. A French traveler, on a sight-seeing trip to Williamsburg, wrote in his diary that he went to the Capitol, where he was "entertained with very strong Debates concerning Duty's that the Parliament wants to lay on the American Colonys, which they call or stile Stamp Dutys." The next day he again "heard very hot Debates." One of the proposed resolves was "that any Person that would offer to sustain that the Parliament of England had a right to impose or lay any Tax or Duty whatsoever on the American Colonys, without the consent of the inhabitants thereof, should be looked upon as a traitor, and deemed an Enemy to his Country."

From contemporary evidence it is clear that the resolutions advocating resistance, which were reported in newspapers, were proposed and debated in the House of Burgesses and defeated in spite of Henry's best thunder and lightning. What did he say? The Frenchman reported that "one of the members stood up and said he had read that in former times Tarquin and Julius had their Brutus, Charles had his Cromwell, and he did not doubt but some good American would stand up in favour of his Country." At this point the Speaker of the House interrupted him, saying that he spoke treason and that one of the loyal burgesses should have stopped him "before he had gone so far."

Other eye-witness descriptions of the speech were written long after the event, when independence had been won and the course of the revolution was being reviewed. Two young men then studying law in Williamsburg often visited the Capitol and observed the legislative process at work—John Tyler, a student of Robert Carter Nicholas, and Thomas Jefferson, a student of George Wythe. That day they stood in the lobby outside the Hall of the House of Burgesses and heard the debates. Tyler's reconstruction of the peroration is a classic example of American oratory almost as familiar as Lincoln's Gettysburg Address. After Henry blasted the Stamp Act as a flagrant example of tyranny, he moved on to forecast its reception in the American colonies. In thrilling and solemn tones he warned: "Tarquin and Caesar had each his Brutus, Charles the First his Cromwell, and George the Third—"

"Treason!" shouted Speaker Robinson. Other cries of "Treason! Treason!" echoed all over the house. Henry, realizing that he had moved too far ahead of his audience, paused until the shouts died down, and then finished the sentence: "And George the Third may profit by their example!"

Jefferson recalled the "most bloody debate" and the "torrents of sublime eloquence from Henry" such as he "never heard from any other man." Here, he seemed to Jefferson "to speak as Homer wrote." While Jefferson did not attempt to reconstruct the climactic phrases, he well remembered "the cry of treason, the pause of Mr. Henry at the name of George III, and the presence of mind with which he closed his sentence, and baffled the charge vociferated."

Paul Carrington, in 1815 the only surviving member of the House of 1765, tried to describe the debate. He could only say that Henry's arguments were "beyond my powers of description," that his "Manly eloquence Surpass'd everything of the kind I had ever heard Before."

After he cleverly finished his sentence, did Henry shout defiantly, "If this be treason, make the most of it"? No one present recalled such an ending. Did he sit down immediately, or did he apologize? According to the Frenchman, he sat down when Speaker Robinson rose to interrupt him; then after Robinson finished speaking, "the same member stood up again (his name is Henery) and said that if he had affronted the speaker, or the house, he was ready to ask pardon." He then protested his loyalty to King George III and explained that his concern for "his Country's Dying liberty" and "the heat of passion" might have led him to say "more than he intended."

In other words, the interruption told him that he had gone too far, that these experienced lawmakers were much more sensitive to hints of disloyalty than the Hanover jury had been, and he knew enough law to understand the penalties for treasonable speech. He used the interval, therefore, to back up gracefully: he had already made his point. Never again in public life would he lose touch with his audience and move too far ahead of it.

News of his Stamp Act performance spread like wildfire. The Frenchman, visiting Newcastle on the Pamunkey a week later, found "nothing talked of but the stamp Dutys" and "a great deal" being said about "the Noble Patriot Mr. Henery, who lives in this County." The inhabitants said "publicly that if the least Injury was offered to him they'd stand by him to the last Drop of their blood."

His critics too were talking. Government officials were offended by his resolves. Governor Fauquier reported: "In the course of the debate, I have heard that very indecent language was used by a Mr. Henry, a young lawyer who had not been above a month a Member of the House" and who carried with him "the young hot and giddy members from the upper counties."

Commissary William Robinson, head of the church in Virginia, informed the Bishop of London of Henry's offensive speech in the "Parsons' Cause" and his subsequent election as burgess for one of the upper counties. In this "character," he "lately distinguished himself in the House of Burgesses on occasion of the arrival of an act of Parliament for stamp duties." He "blazed out in a violent speech against the authority of Parliament and the King, comparing his Majesty to a Tarquin, a Caesar, and a Charles the First, and not sparing insinuations that he wished another Cromwell would arise." Then he had "gone quietly into the upper parts of the country to recommend himself to his constituents by spreading treason and enforcing firm resolutions against the authority of the British Parliament."

Though Henry's name was known in Virginia and in London, in the other colonies the House of Burgesses got all the credit for the denunciation of the Stamp Act. In Boston on June 8 the Massachusetts legislature sent out a circular letter to all the sister colonies proposing a congress to discuss plans for unified protest against the tax. Replies to the invitation were negative until "the publishing of the Virginia resolves proved an alarm Bell to the disaffected," declared Governor Sir Francis Bernard. They "gave the signal for a general out-cry over the continent," said General Thomas Gage in New York, and they changed the attitude of other legislatures. Eight of them passed similar resolves, and nine accepted the invitation of Massachusetts to attend the Stamp Act Congress in New York in October. The congress drew up a declaration of American rights, specifically condemned the Stamp Act, and demanded its repeal. While no Virginia delegates attended the congress (because Fauquier deliberately postponed a meeting of the assembly so that no delegates might be chosen), the influence of the Virginia Resolves may be seen in every phase of the recommendations of the Stamp Act Congress.

Meanwhile, throughout the summer resistance to the Stamp Act was expressed everywhere in riots against the distributors and in defiant "business as usual" without the use of the stamps. In Virginia George Mercer, the stamp collector, was burned in effigy, and when he arrived in Williamsburg with a supply of the stamps, an incipient riot was checked by the courageous action of Governor Fauquier. The outspoken threats of Richard Henry Lee and the pressure of Mercer's friends persuaded him to resign his post. Virginia customs officials continued to give ships clearance papers without the stamps, which were "not available."

In compliance with the act, many of the civil courts closed November 1. British creditors were therefore unable to collect the large annual debts of Virginia planters, who not only stopped paying old accounts but also stopped ordering British goods so long as the tax was in effect. George Washington explained this tactic in a letter to his wife's uncle in London. He had little news, he wrote, because the Stamp Act "engrosses the conversation of the Speculative part of the Colonists, who look upon this unconstitutional method of Taxation as a direful attack upon their Liberties." He expected trade to fall off when Americans should "dispense with Luxuries"; and "if a stop be put to our judicial proceedings I fancy the Merchants of G. Britain trading to the Colonies will not be among the last to wish for a Repeal."

The American boycott did arouse British merchants and manufacturers to exert pressure on the ministry, and in March 1766 the act was repealed.

In retrospect, Henry's oratory in defense of the resolutions may be seen as the opening move in the American Revolution. Jefferson thought that "He was certainly the man who gave the first impulse to the ball of revolution. . . . By these resolutions Mr. Henry took the lead out of the hands of those who had heretofore guided the proceedings of the House, that is to say, of Pendleton, Wythe, Bland, Randolph, Nicholas," honest and able men, "but with a moderation more adapted to their age and experience." As the independence movement grew, "events favored the bolder spirits of Henry, the Lees, Pages, Mason," and Jefferson himself. The two groups learned to work together because they recognized the "importance of unanimity." Although "we often wished to have gone faster," Jefferson explained, "we slackened our pace, that our less ardent colleagues might keep up with us."

Late in life Henry prepared his own estimate of the significance of the Stamp Act Resolves and placed it, along with his will, in a sealed envelope addressed to his executors:

> The resolutions passed the House of Burgesses in May 1765. They formed the first opposition to the Stamp Act and the scheme of taxing America by the British parliament. All the colonies, either through fear, or want of opportunity to form an opposition, or from influence of some kind or other, had remained silent. I had been for the first time elected a Burgess a few days before, was young, inexperienced, unacquainted with the forms of the House, and the members that composed it. Finding the men of weight averse to opposition, and the commencement of the tax at hand, and that no person was likely to step forth, I determined to venture, and alone, unadvised, and unassisted, on a blank leaf of an old law book, wrote the resolutions. Upon offering them to the House violent debates ensued. Many threats were uttered, and much abuse cast on me by the party for submission. After a long and warm contest the resolutions passed by a very small majority, perhaps of one or two only. The alarm spread throughout America with astonishing quickness, and the Ministerial party were overwhelmed. The great point of resistance to British taxation was universally established in the colonies. This brought on the war which finally separated the two countries and gave independence to ours.

III.
Stability, 1766-1774

BACK home in the summer of 1765, Henry returned his attention to private affairs. Though he hated paper work, he kept careful records of accounts with his clients, and parts of his fee books have survived. Along with the legal fees, due or collected, he sometimes jotted down accounts with his overseers and with neighbors who worked for him on the farm and the house. From these sketchy records it is possible to picture his life style in Louisa.

John Gilbert, carpenter, and James Anderson, stone mason, worked on the new house at Roundabout in 1765 and 1766 and had it ready for the family to move into the sturdy building before Christmas. It was a modest dwelling built on conventional lines, with three large rooms and a passageway on the ground floor, and a stairway led to a half-story room above. The building was covered with a shingle roof, and there were chimneys for fireplaces in the downstairs rooms. By modern standards, the house was well filled with a growing family. The eldest daughter Martha, born in 1755, now had two brothers, John and William, and in the summer of 1767 a sister Anne would be born here. In 1767 Anderson made repairs in the cellar and upstairs room.

Like other successful attorneys, Henry took students, and several of them probably lived at Roundabout for brief periods. A young cousin, Isaac Coles, was there in 1767, when he paid twenty pounds for a year's board. William Christian, from Augusta County, studied with Henry at this time and became so well acquainted with his teacher's family that he married Patrick's sister Anne in 1768. Edmund Winston, another cousin, was here in the late 1760's before he became the king's attorney in the new county of Botetourt.

The dwelling house stood on a hillside with a long view down to

Polecat Branch and beyond into the Roundabout Valley, through rolling fields and forests. It was nine miles to Louisa Courthouse, and Henry still enjoyed hunting en route to and from court attendance here and in other counties.

Parts of his 1700 acres were good farmlands. He raised tobacco, corn, wheat, and oats for sale, and his livestock included hogs, sheep, and cattle. Since his law business and public service took him away from home much of the time, he depended on overseers to manage the farm in his absence. William Crane, James Matthews, Joseph Camp, David Melton, and James Hill served him in this capacity from 1764 to 1770. He owned several slaves and hired others from time to time. An indentured servant boy, Thomas White, lived on the place. All these servants worked on the farm, ran errands, sometimes made shoes for the servants or the family, and performed semi-skilled chores in smithing and carpentry.

From time to time Louisa neighbors supplied him with shingles, helped with the reaping, hauled lime for fertilizer, worked in the garden, dressed deerskins, inspected his tobacco, made or mended hogsheads, tubs and other wooden containers. Equipment and supplies were sometimes obtained as fees from merchant clients: cattle, swine, horses, a single horse chair for use in traveling the court circuit, repairs to Sarah's side saddle, a spinning wheel, guns, paint, clothing, "reaping rum" for the harvest feast, and "sundry goods."

While Henry was effecting greater stability in his private affairs, he was given greater responsibilities in community affairs as a member of the vestry of Trinity Parish after the fall of 1765. As though he were acting clerk or churchwarden, in 1766 and 1769 he handled parish funds for taking the poll, checking land boundaries, and caring for the poor.

Much of his law business was concerned with land claims, for boundary disputes were a good source of income for lawyers and surveyors, whether the land was under cultivation or held as an investment. In colonial America, where the chief natural resource was virgin land, speculation in land was the best way to get rich quickly. Tidewater aristocrats usually owed their position to ancestors who came to Virginia in the seventeenth century with enough money to invest in good tobacco lands. By the middle of the eighteenth century the best undeveloped lands lay beyond the piedmont and below the James River. The speculator was required to survey his lands and pay taxes on them (called *quitrents*) while he held them for resale to settlers after they had been "developed." When he could not meet the requirements on time, he might sell part of his holdings to avoid losing all of them.

Henry's legal fees were sometimes paid in undeveloped land claims, and in these circumstances the lawyer easily became a landowner and speculator. When he lent his father £150 in 1764, he received title to the Roundabout farm. In the spring of 1766 his father-in-law, threatened with bankruptcy, employed him to sell some of his western lands. Henry advertised them, but he received no satisfactory offer because the purchaser would have to pay delinquent quitrents and develop the claims. After two years Henry decided to buy about 3400 acres of Shelton's land on the Holston and Clinch rivers. With his brother William, his brother-in-law William Christian, and several others, he made the long trip to Southwest Virginia to locate and inspect the Shelton claims.

Though much of the valley was still Cherokee hunting grounds, it had been surveyed and traveled by other white men; for example, in 1750 Dr. Thomas Walker of Albemarle had traveled the Wilderness Trail from Roanoke to Cumberland Gap, and Daniel Boone was already taking the same route to Kentucky. Henry found a few settlers living in the area, but land titles were clouded by Cherokee claims and by the British Proclamation of 1763, which forbade white settlement beyond the Alleghenies until Indian claims could be adjusted by further negotiation.

Another speculation of Shelton's involved "Mississippi" lands in Kentucky, where the Ohio River joins the Mississippi. This speculation was part of a larger scheme for development in cooperation with more experienced promoters, including Dr. Walker and Capt. James Patton. When Shelton mortgaged his share to his son-in-law in 1768, Henry and Walker employed an agent—Capt. William Fleming of Augusta—to explore the area and prepare a report on the soil, water, timber, grass, and game. The report, if favorable, would then be used in planning a systematic promotional program.

From the failures of John Henry and John Shelton, and from his experience, Patrick Henry developed a good eye for good land and businesslike methods for promoting it, often in association with experienced speculators who would provide part of the capital. For the rest of his life he bought and sold land profitably, in small units which he examined himself, and, as opportunity offered, he invested in the big land companies organized to exploit huge grants in the

21

territory won from France in 1763. Stockholders in these companies—the Ohio, the Loyal, the Vandalia, the Mississippi—included men of influence in London, Virginia, and Pennsylvania.

In the 550 legal fees charged in 1765, collections were improving. Then came November 1, when many county courts closed in protest against the use of stamps on legal documents. Some courts continued to sit regularly to set county taxes and attend to other business that did not require stamps; for example, grand juries met and presented offenders for later trial, or wills and deeds were drawn and held unrecorded. A few counties went ahead with business as usual, ignoring the stamps and gambling on the repeal of the Stamp Act. If the act were not repealed, all regular business done in the lower courts without the stamps could be nullified by the General Court. As a rule, legal business was delayed as much as possible to give Parliament time to respond to the added pressure of British merchants.

The Louisa Court remained closed until May 12, 1766. Ten days earlier news of the repeal was published in the *Virginia Gazette,* but the Louisa justices still insisted that the act was unconstitutional—a position Northhampton County had taken in February. Courts in some of the other counties in which Henry practiced had remained open—Augusta and Cumberland, for example. His fee books pointedly record the slump in legal business: for 1766 he charged fees in 114 cases. In 1767 the number was again normal, 554; by this time Augusta County clients were quite numerous.

The next slump in the number of fees occurred in 1769, when he began to practice in the General Court, the highest court in Virginia, patterned on the House of Lords in England. The governor presided, and the justices were members of the council. The court met in Williamsburg during "Public Times," in April and October, when the little capital was crowded with lawyers, clients, and witnesses waiting for their cases to come up on the court's docket. Most of the business of the court was civil cases appealed from county courts, though trial of disputes involving twenty pounds or more might begin here. Because litigation was said to be a favorite "sport" of colonial Virginians, the docket was always crowded; in order to discourage frivolous appeals, lawyers were not permitted to practice in the county courts and in the high court at the same time. The local legal business of an attorney practicing in the General Court was largely advisory or confined to the paper work of preparing wills, summons, deeds for property sale and transfer.

Important criminal cases—felonies punishable by loss of life or limb—were tried at the end of regular sessions of the General Court or in special "Courts of Oyer and Terminer" held in June and December. For these trials the accused was brought to Williamsburg by his county sheriff, along with neighbors who were to serve on his jury, witnesses and their written testimony, which had been taken down and signed in a special meeting of the county justices, "the Examining Court." In colonial procedure, an accused felon was not often represented by a lawyer; his trial was conducted by the king's attorney in the county, by the attorney general in the General Court, and the accused was permitted to plead his case and question witnesses. Jury and judges then decided whether he was guilty and ordered his release or set the penalty.

The system was generally believed to provide practical justice for the accused because members of the Examining Court were reponsible neighbors who knew him (and the circumstances and the witnesses) well enough to arrive at the truth of the allegations, and they carefully recorded all the testimony for the use of the high court. Since the records of the General Court have not survived, we have no information about the felonies tried there. However, we do have records of many of the examining courts, and newspapers customarily reported the names of convicted felons who were executed. Most of the known felons were indentured servants, accused of robbery, arson, or murder, and indentured servants could not pay lawyers' fees. We know of only one member of the gentry accused of a capital crime—Col. John Chiswell, who died before he could be tried. It seems clear, therefore, that lawyers practicing in the General Court handled only civil cases. This is the reason that Henry's fee books do not record important criminal cases: his great reputation as a criminal lawyer was made after the revolution, in the new state system of justice.

While lawyers pled fewer cases before the General Court, the suits were more important, the fees were larger, and the practice was more prestigious and competitive. In 1769 Henry's rivals there included Pendleton, Wythe, Nicholas, John Blair, Thomson Mason, Jefferson, and the attorney general, John Randolph. The essential qualification for success at the bar of the high court was precise legal argument based on broad knowledge of Virginia law and British constitutional history. Henry quickly mastered these sources. Tradition tells that he asked Pendleton for advice and that Pendleton mapped out a course of study for him and lent him books to follow it through. While there was no place here for flamboyant oratory, persuasive argument won the approval of councilor-justices and of the juries often used in civil cases.

One of Wythe's students, St. George Tucker, first saw Henry in the General Court in April, 1772, under these circumstances: "I attended [the court] very frequently; generally sat near the clerk's table, directly opposite to the bar. I had now for the first time a near view of Mr. Henry's face." He wore the attorney's conventional black suit and tie wig. His visage was long and thin, his profile of a Roman cast. Heavy brows and long black lashes made his blue eyes look dark and piercing. There was nothing remarkable about his mouth, Tucker thought, except its expression: when he wanted to suggest criticism of an opponent's idea, he restated it with a sort of cynical half-smile and made it sound absurd. His manner was modest, dignified, and courteous, and "when he submitted to the *superior wisdom* of the court," he did so "with a grace that would have done honour to the most polished courtier in Westminster Hall." He appeared thoughtful and solemn, and "even on occasions when he excited it in others," he never had "anything like pleasantry in his countenance, his manner, or the tone of his voice. You would swear he had never uttered or laughed at a joke." His voice was pleasant, distinct, and well modulated. He was emphatic but not vehement; animated but never boisterous; nervous but without recourse to intemperate language. And he was always clear.

His fee books sometimes identify appeals, which he pled in the General Court. These clients lived in the counties of Louisa, Buckingham, Goochland, Essex, Amherst and in the cities of Richmond, Norfolk, and Charleston, South Carolina. The suits usually concerned property, but one slander case can be identified. In 1771 for a fee of £2.10 he successfully defended Col. Valentine Wood against Dr. Simeon Harris's charge that the colonel had made "false and defamatory" statements about the doctor's medical qualifications. Surely the cynical half-smile came into play in this case.

The growing respect of rival lawyers was demonstrated by Nicholas in 1773, when he gave up law practice in order to devote full time to his duties as treasurer of the colony: he turned over his clients and their unfinished business to the lawyer from Hanover. Henry's record of good humor, good manners, and a superb sense of timing in association with rivals at the bar made it easier for him to work with them as fellow-burgesses.

Public business took him to Williamsburg in the fall of 1766 for the meeting of the General Assembly, postponed four times since the summer of 1765. He was present November 6 for the organization of the House of Burgesses. Peyton Randolph was chosen speaker, to replace John Robinson, who had died in May. Henry became a member of two of the standing committees, where he might learn the practical details of legislative procedure. Of the seventeen members of the Committee of Privileges and Elections, several had been there in 1764 when Henry appeared before them as counsel for Dandridge—Bland, Richard Henry Lee, Wythe, and Pendleton. Bland chaired the forty-four-member Committee of Propositions and Grievances.

Service on special committees gave a new burgess further opportunity to learn routine procedure, and as time passed, these appointments reflected general attitudes toward his interests and abilities. Henry's appointment to a committee to inquire into the state of the clerk's office was such a routine assignment. More unusual was a twenty-member committee chosen to prepare inscriptions for an obelisk planned to express Virginia's gratitude to "the several noble and worthy Patriots" in both houses of Parliament who distinguished themselves in procuring the repeal of the Stamp Act. The make-up of this group reflected the attitudes of May, 1765: representing the old leadership were Landon Carter, Bland, Wythe, Pendleton, Nicholas, and Speaker Randolph; the new, Henry, Munford, Richard Henry Lee, and Francis Lightfoot Lee.

Another reflection of Henry's performance the year before was his chairmanship of a committee to prepare and deliver an address to the governor respecting bonds issued by the late Treasurer Robinson. In the six months since Robinson's death, the executors of his estate had discovered chaos in his accounts. His friends all over the colony owed the estate £130,000, and about £100,000 of these debts were due to the Treasury of Virginia. The colony had been permitted to issue paper money for a limited time during the French and Indian War; after the emergency was over, the paper was to be called in and destroyed. Then the chronic problem of scarcity of currency became acute in the post-war financial confusion, and Robinson on his own authority as treasurer decided to keep the wartime currency in circulation and lend it to Virginians especially pinched by low tobacco prices; that is, he extended the life of the temporary treasury notes to ease the new emergency. He hoped to balance his accounts through the Loan Office bill, which Henry blocked in 1765. Now in 1766 the treasury books could not be balanced until all these loans were repaid. On December 16 Henry reported to the house that Governor Fauquier had received the address and would order suits against Robinson's estate to begin at once.

Until 1775 Henry continued to work quietly and faithfully in the tedious committee routine of legislative procedure, practicing the dull virtues of patience, competence, and dependability. As he gained experience, he became more useful in special committee assignments; yet he did not achieve the traditional position of leadership symbolized in the chair of one of the great standing committees. Only an exceptional crisis or emotional issue under discussion in the Committee of the Whole House called into play his unique oratorical talents.

The financial problems of the treasurer's office claimed his attention in later sessions. In 1767 the committee examining the accounts recommended, and the house passed, a bill to permit the sale of parts of Robinson's estate. Another special committee drew up an address to the king for permission to issue a new series of paper currency to be redeemed in 1783. In the long winter session of 1769, after the customary examination of the treasurer's accounts, Henry reported the delivery of a new address to Governor Botetourt and presented to the house copies of the current status of suits and collections.

In 1771 Bland, Henry and seven others were asked to inquire into funds for redeeming the paper money issued in the French and Indian War. Finally, in 1772, a new committee prepared a bill for calling in and destroying all the old wartime notes still in circulation. Since Robinson's death, his protégé Pendleton had been in charge of the administration of the estate, a tedious task which would absorb most of his time for fifteen years. He found it necessary to move slowly with the collection of debts in order to avoid throwing too many lands on the market at one time and bankrupting the landed aristocracy. The currency problems were complicated further in 1773, when a group of Pittsylvania counterfeiters were discovered passing forged treasury notes. A burgess from Prince Edward County was suspected, and Henry reported to the house that Governor Dunmore was working with the legislature in the apprehension and trial of the accused counterfeiters.

As early as 1767 Henry was recognized as an authority on frontier lands when he carried a bill to the Council for encouraging the settlement of upper Augusta County. In the fall session of 1769 Bland and Henry were especially active in efforts to persuade Governor Botetourt to take executive action toward the solution of frontier problems. The two Indian agents of the British Crown—John Stuart in the south and Sir William Johnson in the north—had negotiated treaties in 1768 with the Cherokee and the Iroquois. Virginians living on both sides of the Kanawha River were pleased when the Iroquois surrendered title to lands south of the Ohio. But Virginia speculators, represented by Dr. Walker, were not pleased with the Cherokee treaty and wanted it revised. More of the Cherokee hunting grounds, they thought, should be opened to settlement. Dr. Walker persuaded two Cherokee chiefs to give the Virginians the land they wanted, but Stuart and the British ministry disapproved, while Botetourt cooperated with the burgesses. The problems of the control and administration of western lands would not be solved until the Northwest Ordinance of 1787.

The control of the profitable Indian trade gave the crown equally knotty problems. By 1770 the trade was so large that King George III decided to leave its further management to colonial assemblies. Consequently, the legislatures of several colonies chose commissioners to meet in New York to form a cooperative plan to regulate the trade with the Iroquois. On May 30, 1770, the House of Burgesses chose Bland and Henry to join the commissioners from the northern provinces.

The Virginians arrived in New York July 10, but very little business was transacted because the commissioners from Pennsylvania and Quebec did not attend the conference. Bland and Henry returned to Williamsburg the evening of July 18, and the following day the house voted them an additional seventy-five pounds "for their Trouble and Expences." This first trip of Henry's outside Virginia was made in good company, under pleasant traveling conditions, and with an entree to important officials in neighboring colonies; much as he may have enjoyed it, he left posterity not one word about it.

With the repeal of the Stamp Act, pleasant political relations with England were resumed. The Townshend Acts of 1767, another effort to raise revenue in America, put a tax on imports of paints, glass, paper, and tea. These were "external" taxes to which the colonists were not expected to object because they had not questioned Parliament's right to regulate empire trade. But, however disguised, the taxes were for revenue. The money was to be spent in America—not for the protection of the frontiers, but to pay salaries of crown officials and thus free them from the control of colonial legislatures. Commercial New England first condemned the taxes; then other colonies, not so directly affected, objected on principle. At the short session of the Virginia Assembly March 31-April 16, 1768, seventy-five burgesses were absent, including Henry. Governor Fauquier too was absent; he died early in March, and John Blair, president of the Council, presided and permitted the burgesses to protest the Townshend Acts in a petition to George III, a memorial to the House of Lords, and a remonstrance to the House of Commons.

Fauquier's replacement, Norborne Berkeley, Baron de Botetourt, arrived in Virginia in October with instructions to dissolve the assembly and persuade the new one "to desist from their unwarrantable Claims and Pretensions, and yield due submission to the supreme Authority of Parliament." Lord Botetourt accordingly ordered new elections in November and called the assembly to meet the following spring. For some unknown reason this fall Henry stood for election in Hanover instead of Louisa. Jefferson was elected for the first time in Albemarle, and many of the "young hot headed, inexperienced Members" who had alarmed Fauquier were returned from other counties—the Lee brothers, Thomson Mason, Robert Munford among them.

Botetourt was the first titular governor to come to Williamsburg, a friendly and tactful man, determined to restore harmony. He opened the General Assembly May 8, 1769, with style and ceremony. Dressed in a brilliant red coat lavishly trimmed with gold braid, His Lordship left the Palace in a handsome chariot originally designed for George III, now bearing the arms of Virginia. Silver decorated the harness of the six white horses which drew the chariot to the Capitol.

Inside the building everything was dignified, pleasant, and friendly until May 16, when the burgesses adopted resolutions reasserting their exclusive right to levy taxes in Virginia and condemning a recent proposal to revive an old English law which permitted the government to try in London all persons accused of treason. Henry was a member of a special committee of six chosen to express these sentiments in an address to the king. The next day the house adopted the committee's draft of the address, and Botetourt dissolved the assembly.

Immediately most of the burgesses reassembled in the Raleigh Tavern, elected Randolph "moderator" of the meeting, and organized an association to boycott British imports. George Washington had with him a detailed plan for the boycott prepared by his neighbor, George Mason of Gunston Hall, a former burgess as patriotic as his younger brother Thomson but more scholarly and retiring, always reluctant to leave home for public office. On May 18, eighty-eight signers of the Articles of Association, based on Mason's draft, agreed to stop orders for all kinds of British goods until the Townshend duties were removed. The burgesses took copies of the document home with them, and many of their constituents later signed it.

Because the governor had dissolved the legislature, new elections were held in the summer, and the burgesses returned to Williamsburg for the fall session with few changes in membership. On November 7 Lord Botetourt greeted them with news of the repeal of all the Townshend duties except the tax on tea. Once again harmony was restored and the assembly spent forty productive days on routine local affairs. Again Henry was present every day.

The next session, too, worked smoothly from May 21, 1770, until June 28. Enthusiastic support for the Association of 1769 cooled, of course, when the taxes it protested were removed; however, a group of merchants meeting in Williamsburg in June joined burgesses anxious to preserve the boycott machinery, and a new agreement provided for better future enforcement by county committees empowered to publish the names of merchants and others who violated it.

Lord Botetourt died in October, and President William Nelson called the assembly together for ten days in July of 1771 to deal with problems connected with the disastrous spring floods.

Botetourt's successor, John Murray, Earl of Dunmore, arrived in Williamsburg from New York in September and ordered new elections in October. He called his first assembly to meet February 10, 1772. For two months this assembly attended to routine business without interference from the governor or other officials of the crown.

When the next session opened March 4, 1773, the plan to send political offenders to England for trial was being tested in Rhode Island, where a British court of inquiry had been appointed to investigate the burning of the *Gaspée,* a revenue ship. Alarmed at the potential threat to all the colonists, the "forward" young burgesses, led by Henry, the Lee brothers, Jefferson and his brother-in-law

29

Dabney Carr, met privately at the Raleigh for several evenings to work out a program for greater unity of colonial action through systematic exchange of information and plans. Using the Massachusetts town committees as models, they drafted a plan for intercolonial Committees of Correspondence and Inquiry. On March 12 the new member from Louisa, Dabney Carr, presented the plan to the house, Richard Henry Lee and Patrick Henry supported it with their best oratory, the house unanimously adopted it and chose a Virginia committee of eleven members, headed by Speaker Randolph. On March 15 Dunmore prorogued the assembly, and the next day the Committee of Correspondence sent a circular letter to speakers of other colonial legislatures inviting their cooperation.

The response of sister colonies was flattering and enthusiastic. In England the Board of Trade immediately recognized the significance of Virginia's activity and warned the crown of its potential danger to the orderly exercise of royal authority in America. Locally, the committee of correspondence could become a colony's spokesman and administrative agent if the governor should refuse to call the legislature and try to govern by executive action and military force.

While the assembly was still sitting, Parliament blundered again with the Tea Act, which gave the East India Company a monopoly of the American market but at the same time lowered the price because the company sold the tea through their own agents and thus eliminated the middle man, the colonial merchant. Colonial consumers did not react as Parliament expected. Instead of appreciating the bargain price, they resented the forced monopoly and joined merchants and radical patriots in a new boycott. When three tea ships entered the port of Boston in December, a group of Sons of Liberty disguised as Mohawk Indians boarded the ships and dumped the tea into the harbor. Parliament responded with a series of "Intolerable Acts" punishing Massachusetts. The Boston Port Bill ordered the port closed to all commerce after June 1, until the tea was paid for.

The next Virginia assembly met May 5, 1774, and quietly went about its regular business until May 19, when news of the Boston Port Bill appeared in the *Virginia Gazette*. Jefferson, Henry, the Lee brothers, and three or four other young burgesses met privately to decide on a dramatic gesture that would express sympathy with Massachusetts. In the Council Chamber of the Capitol they searched the library for British precedents and "cooked up a resolution" appointing June 1 "a day of fasting, humiliation and prayer, to

HANOVER COURTHOUSE
Courtesy of the Virginia State Library.

ST. JOHN'S CHURCH, RICHMOND.
Courtesy of the Virginia State Chamber of Commerce.

THE SECOND CAPITOL, WILLIAMSBURG, by Howard Pyle, about 1890.
Courtesy of The Colonial Williamsburg Foundation.

SCOTCHTOWN, HANOVER COUNTY.
Courtesy of the Virginia State Library.

THE GOVERNOR'S PALACE, WILLIAMSBURG.
Courtesy of The Colonial Williamsburg Foundation.

RED HILL, CHARLOTTE COUNTY.
Courtesy of the Virginia State Library.

implore heaven to avert from us the evils of civil war, to inspire us with firmness in support of our rights, and to turn the hearts of the King & Parliament to moderation and justice." To ensure conservative support for the resolution, they persuaded Nicholas to present it. On May 24 it passed unanimously. When Dunmore saw a copy of it, he promptly dissolved the house.

The next day eighty-nine burgesses assembled at the Raleigh Tavern and formed a new association to boycott tea and other products of the East India Company. Convinced that "an Attack made on one of our Sister Colonies, to compel Submission to arbitrary Taxes, is an Attack made on all British America, and threatens Ruin to the Rights of all," they asked the Committee of Correspondence to issue a call for an annual congress of representatives from all the colonies "to deliberate on those general measures which the united interests of America may from time to time require."

On May 30 twenty-five burgesses were still in town when a circular letter arrived from Boston proposing a complete boycott of British goods; they immediately called a convention to meet in Williamsburg August 1 to consider the proposal.

As in May 1765, so in May 1774 Henry played a leading political role. George Mason, who was in Williamsburg on private business, found everyone's attention "engrossed by the Boston affair." Measures "intended for the preservation of our rights and liberties" were being planned, Mason noticed, "with a great deal of privacy, and by a very few members, of whom Patrick Henry is the principal." At the request of several friends, Mason joined them one evening, when he "had an opportunity of conversing with Mr. Henry and knowing his sentiments." In Mason's judgment, Henry was "by far the most powerful speaker" he ever heard. Yet "his eloquence is the smallest part of his merit. He is in my opinion the first man on this continent, as well in abilities as public virtues."

During the summer, counties not only endorsed the principles of the association and elected delegates to the August convention but also expressed sympathy for Boston with resolutions of support and practical gifts of money and supplies. The county resolutions often spoke with the voices of the young burgesses chosen delegates to the convention: in Fairfax County, Washington and Mason; in Albemarle, Jefferson; in Hanover, Henry.

When the First Virginia Convention met in Williamsburg August 1, it formally endorsed Boston's proposal and agreed to refuse all

British imports after November 1 and to stop all exports—even tobacco—after August 10, 1775. Then seven delegates were chosen to represent Virginia at the Continental Congress in Philadelphia in September: Speaker Randolph, Richard Henry Lee, Washington, Henry, Bland, Harrison, and Pendleton.

Leaving Williamsburg August 6, Henry hurried back to Hanover to attend to private affairs at his new plantation, Scotchtown, which he had purchased about 1771. The house, his most elegant residence, had been built by Col. John Chiswell's father, a Scotsman. After 1760 it belonged to Chiswell's son-in-law, Speaker Robinson, and Henry was able to buy the house and 960 acres of land at a bargain price, £600, because it was part of Robinson's estate put up for quick sale.

Scotchtown was a rectangular building ninety-four feet by thirty-six, with a tall brick chimney at each end and stone steps leading to the front door. On the first floor were eight rooms and a large central hall, some of them paneled or wainscotted in walnut or mahogany. A large attic extended over all the first floor, and there were eight rooms and a wine cellar in the basement. The imposing mansion house was surrounded by a white paling fence, and the grounds were decorated with boxwood and other shrubs and shaded by oaks and other trees. Outbuildings included a kitchen, wash house, blacksmith shop, and storage facilities. Down the hill out of sight were servants' quarters and a mill. Like Henry's other residences, Scotchtown commanded a panoramic view, and there were woodlands nearby. Much of the farmland was already under cultivation in Chiswell's day, and Henry would increasingly depend on farm income as the revolution advanced; his law business declined after the General Court closed in 1774, and his growing involvement in public service made great demands upon his time.

After three weeks at home, Henry set out for Philadelphia, stopping the first night at Mount Vernon, where Pendleton and George Mason were also guests. Wednesday afternoon, May 31, Mason went home and the three delegates began their four-day journey, arriving in Philadelphia just in time for the opening of the congress on Monday, September 5.

About half of the fifty-two delegates had been in town long enough to become friends, for the City of Brotherly Love welcomed them with ceremony and entertained them lavishly. The other four Virginians—Randolph, Harrison, Bland, and Lee—had arrived on Friday, and the men from Massachusetts had been there a week. John

Adams took time out from the festivities to make long entries in his diary, describing the delegates and the atmosphere of their work and play. He was especially interested in the delegates from Virginia, the largest colony and the best friend of Massachusetts: "more sensible, fine fellows you would never wish to see." The Virginians were often to be seen at the home of Dr. William Shippen, Lee's brother-in-law and host, who was equally pleased with them.

Henry was staying at the City Tavern, where the delegates met on Monday and decided to hold their sessions in the long room at Carpenters' Hall. First, by unanimous vote, they chose Randolph chairman. Then they tackled the touchy question of how they would count votes—by colony, by poll, or by some system that would take into account the size of each colony. James Duane of New York proposed that a committee be appointed to decide the method of voting. Henry "then rose, and said this was the first general congress which had ever happened; that no former congress could be a precedent; that we should have occasion for more general congresses, and therefore that a precedent ought to be established now." He endorsed Duane's proposal because, in his opinion, "it would be a great injustice if a little colony should have the same weight in the councils of America as a great one."

No action was taken that day, and on Tuesday the discussion continued. Again Henry spoke first. By the oppression of Parliament, he declared, all government is dissolved. Fleets and armies and the present state of things show that government is dissolved, and colonial boundaries are no longer significant, for we are in a state of nature. Without accurate statistical information, it is impossible to draw up a graduated scale of the relative weight of each colony, and all America is thrown into one mass. "The distinctions between Virginians, Pennsylvanians, New Yorkers, and New Englanders are no more," he concluded. "I am not a Virginian, but an American."

What did he mean? Not what some of his admirers have said, that he became a nationalist overnight, for he would always think of himself as a Virginian, and when he said "my country," he meant "Virginia." Nor had he shifted his position on voting procedure. Rather, he shifted the grounds of the argument for proportionate representation. If, in the state of nature, the old boundaries had disappeared, then the delegates could not be counted by colony because distinctions between the colonies would have disappeared; if each delegate represented a certain number of "Americans," then numbers would have to be the basis for voting strength. In short, his eloquent appeal for unanimity of thought and action had a sting in its tail.

Though rights based on a state of nature was one of the most popular talking points of the day and would be used here at the congress later in the session, Henry's colleagues did not accept it in his context. Harrison bluntly argued that his constituents expected him to see that voting strength be set up according to relative size, and he prophesied that if the New Englanders should "put upon his Country" the "disrespect" of equal representation, the other delegates might never see Virginians at another convention. Lee and Bland wanted proportionate representation but doubted that a committee could draw up an accurate scale. Thomas Lynch of South Carolina thought that property ought to receive equal weight with population in determining the scale. Pendleton did not agree with Henry that boundaries had disappeared, and he argued that a committee might assemble temporary estimates of population and property on which to base a temporary scale and thus set the desired precedent. John Jay of New York agreed with Pendleton, that all government was not at an end, and argued that the congress was meeting to correct errors in the old system, not to create a new government. Samuel Ward of Rhode Island insisted that the weakest colony had as much at stake as the greatest and embarrassed the Virginia delegates with the observation that Virginia counties of unequal size had equal voice in the General Assembly.

By the end of the day no one had offered a satisfactory formula. Most of the delegates were tired of the argument and eager to move on to discussion of the issues on the agenda. They decided against further delay, which a committee would require, and passed a resolution "that in determining questions in this Congress, each colony or province shall have one vote; the Congress not being possessed of, or at present able to procure, proper materials for ascertaining the importance of each colony." Though the smaller colonies won the day, the congress was careful to declare that they were not setting a precedent for future conventions. However, the larger colonies would not get proportionate representation until the Constitution went into effect in 1789.

Once the voting procedure was determined, the congress moved on to the business which their constituents had sent them to do. For seven weeks they assembled at nine each morning and worked steadily until three. The meetings were secret, and the secretary did not record all the discussions, only decisions. At about four in the afternoon the delegates dined and then spent the evening in group discussions or in formal entertainment by Pennsylvania officials or Philadelphia citizens.

Organized like a legislature, the congress worked largely through committees. On September 7 two important committees were chosen: a small group, composed of one member from each colony, to report on the British statutes regulating trade and manufactures; a larger group, composed of two members from each colony, to draw up a statement of the rights of the colonies. Henry represented Virginia in the first group; Lee and Pendleton in the second. The Committee on Statutes presented their report September 17, and Henry was added to the Committee on Rights, where lively discussions continued another week.

Two important state papers were written by other committees. Henry helped to prepare the address to the king, and Lee, the address to the people of Great Britain. The high quality of the statesmanship of these papers was greatly admired, even in Parliament.

On September 28 Joseph Galloway of Pennsylvania proposed a Plan of Union for the colonies which would give them an American legislature elected by colonial assemblies (like the Continental Congress) and a president general chosen by the king. As in the "home rule" set up in the later British Empire, in this plan the president general had a veto and Parliament retained some control of the American legislature. Though most of the delegates, like their constituents, talked about their desire for conciliation with Great Britain, only the middle colonies approved Galloway's plan; New England and the South together defeated it. Both Henry and Lee spoke against it because they did not believe that England would ever give the American colonies real home rule. Nor were they willing to trust Virginia's interests to the control of a national legislature; they would oppose the Constitution fifteen years later for the same reason.

When Galloway presented his plan, the congress had already endorsed a series of resolutions adopted in Suffolk County, Massachusetts, recommending complete cessation of trade with Great Britain until the rights of the colony were restored. With the repeal of the Stamp and Townshend acts in mind, the congress hoped that a new boycott would have the same effect on the Intolerable Acts. The

Continental Association of 1774, patterned on Virginia's, used the same machinery for enforcement: a committee in each county, city, and town would exert whatever pressures were needed, from publicity to tar and feathers.

When the Continental Congress adjourned October 26, Lee and Washington were the only Virginia delegates still in Philadelphia. Three days earlier the others began the journey home in order to be in time for the November meeting of the General Assembly. On the whole, they were pleased with the achievements of the Congress and with their own participation in them. Adams, after talking with all of them, found slight disparities in their attitudes. Lee was convinced that the Intolerable Acts would be repealed, the army and fleet would be recalled, and all American grievances would be redressed. Washington thought the association might be effective if non-importation, non-use, and non-exportation were enforced everywhere. Henry feared that it might become necessary to oppose Parliament with armed force.

Henry and Lee commanded special attention in committee and on the floor. Silas Deane of Connecticut expressed the general impression when he wrote to his wife: "Mr. Henry . . . is the completest speaker I ever heard; but in a letter I can give you no idea of the music of his voice, or the high wrought yet natural elegance of his style and manner. Col. Lee is said to be his rival in eloquence, and in Virginia and to the Southward they are styled the Demosthenes and Cicero of America. God grant they may not, like them, plead in vain for the liberties of their country!"

IV.

The Idol of Virginia, 1775-1776

DURING the autumn months the boycott became effective everywhere except in Georgia, which had not sent delegates to the congress. Yet English merchants did not immediately feel the full force of the pressure because of increased exports to southern Europe and to East India. By the end of the year, in every Virginia county a committee was vigorously enforcing the association. "Every County, besides," Lord Dunmore reported, "is now Arming a Company of Men, whom they call an independent Company for the avowed purpose of protecting their Committees, and to be employed against Government if occasion require." Though the governor exaggerated their numbers, many counties followed the example of Hanover, where Henry organized a company of volunteers early in November.

Dunmore continued to postpone the next session of the assembly, and in January 1775 the counties elected delegates to a second convention, to meet at Richmond so that the governor might not break it up. Because Richmond was only a village, it had no public building large enough to accommodate the convention, and the delegates assembled at Henrico Parish Church, later named St. John's Church, Monday, March 20. Once again Peyton Randolph presided.

First, the convention approved the work of the Continental Congress and thanked the seven delegates for their services there. On Thursday, Patrick Henry—tired of waiting for the king's reply to the address of the Continental Congress sent off six months earlier—introduced resolutions to approve and systematize the formation of independent companies. Maryland had already made arrangements for armed resistance; in November their convention recommended that all Marylanders between the ages of sixteen and fifty be armed and drilled. Henry's resolutions borrowed some of Maryland's phrases but proposed a more moderate preparedness:

> *Resolved,* That a well-regulated militia, composed of gentlemen and yeomen, is the natural strength and only security of a free government; that such a militia in this colony would forever render it unnecessary for the mother country to keep among us for the purpose of our defence any standing army of mercenary forces ... and would obviate the pretext of taxing us for their support. ...
> *Resolved,* therefore, That this colony be immediately put into a posture of defence. ...

Richard Henry Lee seconded the motion, Jefferson and others spoke in support of it. Bland, Harrison, and Pendleton thought it reckless to give the convention's public sanction to the unofficial activities of the counties when King and Parliament might yet make a favorable response.

Henry's oratory in support of his motion has come down to us as an uninterrupted speech:

> No man, Mr. President, thinks more highly than I do of the patriotism, as well as the abilities, of the very honorable gentlemen who have just addressed the House. But different men often see the same subject in different lights; and, therefore, I hope it will not be thought disrespectful of those gentlemen if, entertaining, as I do, opinions of a character very opposite to theirs, I should speak forth my sentiments freely, and without reserve. This is no time for ceremony. The question before the house is one of awful moment to this country. For my own part, I consider it as nothing less than a question of freedom or slavery. And in proportion to the magnitude of the subject ought to be the freedom of the debate. It is only in this way that we can hope to arrive at truth, and fulfil the great responsibility which we hold to God and our country. Should I keep back my opinions at such a time, through fear of giving offence, I should consider myself as guilty of treason towards my country, and of an act of disloyalty towards the majesty of Heaven, which I revere above all earthly kings.
> Mr. President, it is natural to man to indulge in the illusions of Hope. We are apt to shut our eyes against a painful truth, and listen to the song of that siren till she transforms us into beasts. Is this the part of wise men, engaged in a great and arduous struggle for liberty? Are we disposed to be of the number of those who, having eyes, see not, and having ears, hear not, the things which so nearly

44

concern their temporal salvation? For my part, whatever anguish of spirit it may cost, I am willing to know the whole truth; to know the worst, and to provide for it.

I have but one lamp by which my feet are guided, and that is the lamp of experience. I know of no way of judging of the future but by the past. And, judging by the past, I wish to know what there has been in the conduct of the British ministry, for the last ten years, to justify those hopes with which gentlemen have been pleased to solace themselves and the House. Is it that insidious smile with which our petition has been lately received? Trust it not, sir; it will prove a snare to your feet. Suffer not yourselves to be betrayed with a kiss. Ask yourselves how this gracious reception of our petition comports with those warlike preparations which cover our waters and darken our land. Are fleets and armies necessary to a work of love and reconciliation? Have we shown ourselves so unwilling to be reconciled, that force must be called in to win back our love? Let us not deceive ourselves, sir. These are the implements of war and subjugation,—the last arguments to which kings resort.

I ask gentlemen, sir, what means this martial array, if its purposes be not to force us to submission? Can gentlemen assign any other possible motive for it? Has Great Britain any enemy in this quarter of the world, to call for all this accumulation of navies and armies? No, sir, she has none. They are meant for us: they can be meant for no other. They are sent over to bind and rivet upon us those chains which the British ministry have been so long forging.

And what have we to oppose to them? Shall we try argument? Sir, we have been trying that for the last ten years. Have we anything new to offer upon the subject? Nothing. We have held the subject up in every light of which it is capable; but it has been all in vain. Shall we resort to entreaty, and humble supplication? What terms shall we find which have not been already exhausted?

Let us not, I beseech you, sir, deceive ourselves longer. Sir, we have done everything that could be done to avert the storm which is now coming on. We have petitioned; we have remonstrated; we have supplicated; we have prostrated ourselves before the throne, and have implored its interposition to arrest the tyrannical hands of the ministry and Parliament. Our petitions have been slighted; our remonstrances have produced additional violence and insult; and we have been spurned with contempt from the foot of the throne.

In vain, after these things, may we indulge the fond hope

of peace and reconciliation. There is no longer any room for hope. If we wish to be free; if we mean to preserve inviolate those inestimable privileges for which we have been so long contending; if we mean not basely to abandon the noble struggle in which we have been so long engaged, and which we have pledged ourselves never to abandon until the glorious object of our contest shall be obtained,—we must fight! I repeat it, sir,—we must fight! An appeal to arms, and to the God of hosts, is all that is left us.

Thus far, wrote St. George Tucker, Henry spoke with the "calm dignity of Cato of Utica." Then, as he moved into his peroration, his own emotion gradually deepened in manner, voice, and gesture:

They tell us, sir, that we are weak,—unable to cope with so formidable an adversary. But when shall we be stronger? Will it be the next week, or the next year? Will it be when we are totally disarmed, and when a British guard shall be stationed in every house? Shall we gather strength by irresolution and inaction? Shall we acquire the means of effectual resistance by lying supine on our backs, and hugging the delusive phantom of Hope, until our enemies shall have bound us hand and foot?

Sir, we are not weak, if we make proper use of those means which the God of nature hath placed in our power. Three millions of people armed in the holy cause of liberty, and in such a country as that which we possess, are invincible by any force which our enemy can send against us.

Besides, sir, we shall not fight our battles alone. There is a just God who presides over the destinies of nations, and who will raise up friends to fight our battles for us. The battle, sir, is not to the strong alone; it is to the vigilant, the active, the brave. Besides, sir, we have no election. If we were base enough to desire it, it is now too late to retire from the contest. There is no retreat but in submission and slavery. Our chains are forged. Their clanking may be heard on the plains of Boston. The war is inevitable. And let it come! I repeat it, sir, let it come!

It is in vain, sir, to extenuate the matter. Gentlemen may cry peace, peace, but there is no peace. The war is actually begun. The next gale that sweeps from the north will bring to our ears the clash of resounding arms. Our brethren are already in the field. Why stand we here idle? What is it that gentlemen wish? what would they have? Is life so dear, or peace so sweet, as to be purchased at the price of chains and slavery? Forbid it, Almighty God! I know not what course others may take, but as for me, give me liberty, or give me death!

46

In the convention's silent tribute to the orator's dramatic power, one listener thought of St. Paul preaching at Athens; another "felt sick with excitement" and the men around him seemed to be "beside themselves"; another, seated in the window, leaped to the ground and cried, "Let me be buried at this spot!"

The motion passed, and Henry was chosen chairman of a committee of twelve to prepare a plan for "embodying, arming, and disciplining" the militia. Henry thought two regiments (about a thousand men) would be adequate. Nicholas argued that ten or twenty thousand would be needed. The committee recommended "one or more volunteer companies of infantry and troops of horse in each county" to be "in constant training and readiness to act on any emergency." These companies were to be outside the control of the governor and responsible instead to the county committees.

Henry belonged to another committee, chosen to prepare a plan for the encouragement of arts and manufactures. Necessities normally imported from Great Britain included salt and the basic materials for war—guns, ammunition, powder. Already scarcities were being felt everywhere, and local manufactures would become increasingly important in wartime.

With other lawyers—Bland, Jefferson, Nicholas, Pendleton—Henry inquired into the legality of the king's proposal to change the procedure for granting lands. If war should come, Virginia might have to defend her western lands against Indians friendly to the British, against Canadians and other colonies as well as the big land companies.

Finally, the convention chose delegates to the Second Continental Congress, to meet in May. The first seven names on the list were Randolph, Washington, Henry, Richard Henry Lee, Pendleton, Harrison, and Bland; alternates included Jefferson, Thomas Nelson, and Francis Lightfoot Lee.

About a month after the convention delegates left Richmond, a crisis occurred in Williamsburg, where the colony's supply of ammunition, gunpowder, guns, and other military equipment was stored in the Powder Magazine. During the night of April 20-21 a group of royal marines under Dunmore's order secretly moved the barrels of powder from the magazine to the *Fowey*, a man-of-war stationed in Hampton Roads. When the loss was discovered, drums sounded the alarm and Williamsburg citizens gathered at Market Square to threaten the governor. (This enterprise was the Virginia equivalent of the Massachusetts action at Lexington and Concord two days earlier.) Violence was avoided when Randolph, Nicholas, and the mayor persuaded the mob to send a delegation to the Palace with a formal request for the return of the powder.

News of the incident quickly spread all over Virginia, and volunteer companies from the northern and western counties began to assemble at Fredericksburg for a march on Williamsburg. But before the march began, cooler heads among the officers sent an advance agent to the capital to report on the situation there. The messenger returned to Fredericksburg with the news that all was quiet in Williamsburg and brought a letter from Randolph urging the men to go home. Randolph's advice was followed.

In Hanover County Henry summoned the county committee to meet on May 2 at Newcastle; there he persuaded the volunteers to begin their own independent march on Williamsburg to force Dunmore to return the powder or pay for it. They camped at Doncastle's Ordinary about fifteen miles out of Williamsburg, where they were met by Carter Braxton carrying a draft for £330 of public money which was to be used to buy powder and ammunition. When Nicholas refused Henry's offer to go on into town and guard the treasury, Henry dismissed his men and hurried off to Philadelphia. He paused along the way to acknowledge plaudits from his admirers, and he was accompanied by an armed escort and followed by a kind of accolade—Dunmore's proclamation declaring him an outlaw.

At the Second Continental Congress Henry found the same conservative attitudes, the same procedures, and most of the same members as in the First. One of the new members was Benjamin Franklin, who returned from England in time to replace Galloway. This summer the delegates met in the State House (now called Independence Hall). They worked longer hours and devoted less time to entertainment.

The most important question on the agenda was how the congress, a provisional government without constitutional authority, could organize, finance, and fight an undeclared war. At the request of Massachusetts the congress took charge of the American troops at Boston and authorized six companies of expert riflemen from western Virginia and other colonies to serve there immediately. To finance the Continental Army, they authorized a war chest of two million dollars, the money to be raised by printing currency backed by the good will of individual colonies; the congress had no authority to raise money by taxation. Men and supplies were requisitioned from each colony.

After long discussion, on June 16 Washington was unanimously chosen commander-in-chief. Hardly anyone outside New England was enthusiastic about this choice, for more experienced professional soldiers were available. But Washington was a Southerner, and Bostonians hoped that his appointment would encourage intercolonial support for their war. Pendleton and other Virginians understood the political implications of the appointment and hesitated to commit their colony irrevocably to the radical New England course of action.

The majority of the delegates still hoped for reconciliation with England. Therefore, they prepared the customary statement of the rights of the colonies and yet another series of addresses to the king, to the people of Great Britain, Jamaica, Ireland, and to the American Indians—all intended to win support in the contest with Parliament and the ministry.

Randolph left Philadelphia in time to preside over the House of Burgesses on June 1, when the first General Assembly since May of 1774 met in Williamsburg. He was replaced in the chair by John Hancock and in the Virginia delegation by Jefferson. Most of the other Virginians stayed on until adjournment on August 1, for a month's recess. Henry started home on Sunday, July 30, taking with him a difficult committee assignment for the recess—to produce or procure lead and salt for the use of the Continental Army.

Thus Henry missed the meeting of the burgesses, who approved the work of the county committees and volunteers. However, the assembly was unable to pass any legislation. When Dunmore fled the Palace the second week in June and set up headquarters aboard the *Fowey,* all further communication between legislature and executive was by messenger. Fearing that the governor would carry out his threat to pillage the tidewater, the Third Convention met in Richmond July 17 in order to deal with the expected raids.

First, they elected officers for the new regiments. Like the similar election in the Continental Congress, the contest became political. Henry's friends insisted that he was willing to serve and that he had all the qualities needed for military leadership. Others questioned his military qualifications. The march to Doncastle's Ordinary was his only military experience, and more experienced officers were at hand. Hugh Mercer of Fredericksburg, a Scottish officer at Culloden and a captain under Braddock, was a hero of several frontier engagements against the Indians and at Fort Duquesne. William Woodford of Caroline County, a friend of Pendleton, had also fought well in the French and Indian War.

On the first ballot Mercer received forty-one votes, Henry forty, Thomas Nelson eight, Woodford one. On the second ballot August 5, Henry was chosen commander-in-chief of the Virginia forces and colonel of the First Regiment. Woodford became colonel of the Second Regiment, Mercer a brigadier general in Washington's army, and Nelson a member of the Continental Congress.

The tempo of activity in the convention picked up with the arrival of delegates from Philadelphia: Henry, Pendleton, Jefferson, and Harrison on August 9, Lee and Bland two days later. To finance the provisional government, the convention authorized paper money, to be redeemed later by regular taxes. Ordinances were passed to purchase arms and ammunition, saltpeter, sulphur, and lead; also a "manufactory" of arms was set up near Fredericksburg under the management of Fielding Lewis, Washington's brother-in-law. New delegates to the Continental Congress were chosen to replace Henry, Pendleton, and Bland: Francis Lightfoot Lee, Thomas Nelson, and George Wythe.

With Dunmore absent from the capital, the colony had no executive and the General Assembly could not meet. Although the convention was acting as a provisional government, some executive authority was needed to act while the convention was not in session, to perform the day-to-day functions of government and prepare for war. Traditionally in this kind of emergency a dictator is chosen, but Dunmore's behavior made Virginians suspicious of executive power, and the convention gave extraordinary emergency powers to an executive committee. The eleven members of this Committee of Safety were Pendleton, Mason, Page, Bland, Thomas Ludwell Lee, Paul Carrington, and five others. A quorum of six was empowered to do anything it considered necessary in the periods between meetings of the convention.

When Henry returned to Scotchtown at the end of August, family problems awaited him. Sarah Henry had not been well for some time, "extremely ill" in the fall of 1774 with what we would diagnose today as a nervous breakdown. No one recorded the date or circumstances of her death, which occurred in the early spring or late summer of

1775. The eldest daughter Martha, now married to John Fontaine, assumed the care of her sisters and brothers (Anne, Elizabeth, John, William, and four-year-old Edward) either in her husband's house or at Scotchtown, where farming operations continued under the management of an agent.

On September 21, 1775, "Patrick Henry, Commander-in-chief of the Virginia Forces," arrived in Williamsburg. The *Virginia Gazette* reported that "He was met and escorted to town by the whole body of volunteers, who paid him every mark of respect and distinction in their power." After a tour of inspection, he chose a camp site behind the College of William and Mary and set about the organization of the motley troops arriving daily, many of them inadequately equipped and trained. For uniforms they wore hunting shirts. The two companies of expert marksmen brought their own rifles. The most colorful unit in the little army was a battalion from Culpeper County which flew the rattlesnake flag with the motto "Don't tread on me." Dressed in green hunting shirts with the words "Liberty or Death" emblazoned on their chests, they wore buck tails in their hats and carried tomahawks and scalping knives in their belts.

By mid-October about a thousand volunteers had arrived, enough men to fill two regiments, and more recruits were available. The Committee of Safety, through their commissary officers, was at work finding arms and supplies for them. By the end of October all the men from the temporary encampment were quartered in the town, either in public buildings or in private homes. A letter from Mayor William Pasteur, speaking for the citizens of the town, offered Colonel Henry "most sincere and unfeigned thanks" for his "care and vigilence" to "keep up the most precise order and discipline among the troops now quartered here under his command, the good effects whereof we have already abundantly experienced." Henry achieved this degree of public morale through persuasion—in newspaper notices, in speeches to the troops, and in private talks with his soldiers. For formal military training, he had the assistance of an experienced lieutenant-colonel, William Christian, his brother-in-law.

Dunmore's expected attack on Williamsburg did not take place; instead, Norfolk and Portsmouth were threatened, and the Committee of Safety decided to send the Second Regiment to protect the coastal towns. Pendleton, chairman of the committee, informed Colonel Henry of the decision and requested his cooperation in providing additional men and supplies from the First Regiment, but the commander-in-chief of the Virginia forces was not consulted when Woodford was given the independent command and instructed to report directly to the committee. While Henry remained inactive in winter quarters, Woodford won all the glory of the first Virginia victory at Great Bridge. When reinforcements from North Carolina joined the Second Virginia Regiment, the Carolinian Col. Robert Howe was given command of the combined forces at Norfolk.

The Fourth Virginia Convention assembled in Richmond December 1 and the next day moved to Williamsburg. Randolph had recently died, and Pendleton replaced him as president of the convention. Though Pendleton was now the most powerful man in Virginia, Henry was the most popular, and his friends in the convention joined his soldiers in resentment of his "ill treatment." Pendleton had no particular animus for Henry, though he often opposed him in politics; he simply did not trust his political judgment or his military competence. The new Committee of Safety, chosen December 16, was headed by Henry's friends: Digges, Page, Carrington, with Pendleton fourth instead of first on the list. The new committee passed a ruling that Woodford, while acting under "separate and detached command," ought to report to Henry and accept his orders when neither the committee nor the convention was sitting.

The Continental Congress in February organized the six Virginia regiments requested the preceding summer for the continental service, and the First and Second were included in the six. Henry was offered a colonelcy in the Continental Army. When he refused the offer and returned to civilian life, his friends were convinced that the machinations of political opponents had kept him out of a brilliant military career.

When his troops heard that he "was about to leave them," they "went into deep mourning, and being under arms, waited on him at his lodgings" and delivered a farewell address, which was reported verbatim in the *Virginia Gazette*. Being "deeply impressed" with their sense of obligation for his "polite, humane, and tender treatment," they offered "sincere thanks, as the only tribute in our power to pay to your real merits." Though his withdrawal from the service filled them "with the most poignant sorrow," they applauded his "spirited resentment to the most glaring indignity. May your merit," they concluded, "shine as conspicuous to the world in general as it hath done to us, and may Heaven shower its choicest blessings upon you."

Henry expressed suitable appreciation of their loyalty, complimented them on their "spirit, alacrity, and zeal," and declared: "I am unhappy to part with you. I leave the service, but I leave my heart with you. May God bless you, and give you success and safety, and make you the glorious instruments of saving our country."

Then the officers insisted that he dine with them at the Raleigh Tavern. After dinner, ready to give him a military escort out of town, they found a large group of soldiers "assembled in a tumultuous manner," demanding their discharge, and "declaring their unwillingness to serve under any other commander." Whereupon, "Col. Henry found it necessary to stay a night longer in town, which he spent in visiting the several barracks, and used every argument in his power with the soldiery to lay aside their imprudent resolution, and to continue in the service." He explained his own resignation "from motives in which his honour alone was concerned" and promised to "exert his utmost abilities" in the "interest of the united colonies, in support of the glorious cause in which they are engaged." His arguments, "accompanied with the extraordinary exertions of Col. Christian and the other officers present, happily produced the desired effect," and the editor was able to assure the public "that those brave fellows are now pretty well reconciled, and will spend the last drop of their blood in their country's defence."

After Patrick Henry, private citizen, left Williamsburg, he heard everywhere two topics of discussion closely touching his interests. Friends, as indignant as his soldiers, declared their support and criticized the Committee of Safety and the Continental Congress in conversation and in the press. "An honest Farmer" suggested: "From the great man's amiable disposition, his invariable perseverance in the cause of liberty, we apprehend that envy strove to bury in obscurity his martial talents." Understandably dissatisfied "with only an empty title, the mere echo of authority," he was expected to resume his place in Philadelphia, where "his superior abilities . . . could be exerted . . . for his country's good." The Hanover electors early in April decided what he should do next by sending him to the Fifth Virginia Convention.

The burning question in everyone's thoughts that spring was, What are we fighting for? In January Thomas Paine's *Common Sense* offered so convincing an answer—separation—that within a few months the pamphlet sold 100,000 copies. Early in February extensive excerpts were printed in all three *Virginia Gazettes,* and in almost every succeeding issue letters to the editor endorsed Paine's common-sense answer. Many counties, when they elected delegates to the May convention, instructed them how to vote on the most important question on the agenda.

While the majority wanted, separation, there was considerable difference of opinion about practical details of timing a formal declaration of independence. If one colony were to take the initiative, what assurance was there that the others would follow? Should each colony declare separately, or should the Continental Congress speak for all? A successful war with Great Britain would require an ally with a strong navy; should an alliance with France or Spain be negotiated before the declaration? If a general war should develop, would the Continental Congress be able to manage it, or would a more permanent, constitutional union be required?

The 128 delegates to the convention assembled in Williamsburg May 6. Richard Henry Lee, Jefferson, and Wythe were in Philadelphia, but the other leaders were present, and new members included James Madison and Edmund Randolph. Though friends of Henry nominated Thomas Ludwell Lee as president, Pendleton was elected and quickly organized the convention for long hours of work. Committees met at seven a.m., reported to the house at ten, and usually resumed work in the evening. Henry was a member of all the important committees.

After attending to the urgent business of governing a colony at war, the convention went into the Committee of the Whole on May 14 to consider the state of the colony. During two days of discussion, three or more resolutions concerning relations with Great Britain were considered. One recommended separation and proposed a committee to prepare a Declaration of Rights and a new Plan of Government. Another declared Virginians "discharged from any allegiance to the crown of Great Britain." Henry's resolution, the third, proclaimed Virginians "absolved of our allegiance to the crown of Great Britain and obliged by the eternal laws of self-preservation to pursue such measures as may conduce to the good and happiness of the united colonies." It recommended that "our delegates in Congress be enjoined in the strongest and most positive manner to exert their ability in procuring an immediate, clear, and full Declaration of Independency."

None of these resolutions mentioned the question most hotly debated, the timing of a declaration in relation to united colonial action and foreign alliance. Henry's insipid language and restrained

54

position reflected his doubts about timing. From letters from Philadelphia in April he learned that the prevailing opinion in the congress favored securing allies before declaring independence. Richard Henry Lee urged an immediate alliance, before Great Britain could offer France or Spain pieces of American territory as rewards for neutrality or active help in the defeat of the rebellious colonies. Carter Braxton pointed out the importance of a strong naval power as an ally.

Among the proponents of an immediate declaration was General Charles Lee, since late March stationed in Williamsburg in command of the Southern Department of the Continental Army. In flattering conversations and letters, he urged Henry to use his "great influence" and "transcendent abilities" to push a declaration through the convention. Lee told him confidentially that a secret committee of the congress had felt the pulse of French and Spanish agents and found them favorable to an alliance, which would supply immediate help after independence was declared; that delay of "a whole year," which formal negotiations would require, would be fatal.

After two days of debate, Pendleton offered a compromise resolution:

> That the delegates appointed to represent this colony in General Congress be instructed to propose to that respectable body to declare the United Colonies free and independent states, absolved from all allegiance to, or dependence upon, the crown or parliament of Great Britain; and that they give the assent of this colony to such declaration, and to whatever measures may be thought proper and necessary by the Congress for forming foreign alliances, and a confederation of the colonies, at such time, and in the manner, as to them shall seem best: Provided, that the power of forming government for, and the regulations of the internal concerns of each colony, be left to the respective colonial legislatures.

Like all good compromises, this one pleased no one but included everyone's reservations. Edmund Randolph credited Henry with its unanimous acceptance. Speaking on May 15, he "entered into no subtlety of reasoning" but voiced "the now apparent spirit of the people" for independence, a spirit like "a pillar of fire, which notwithstanding the darkness of the prospect would conduct to the promised land." He "inflamed, and was followed by, the Convention." The British Great Union flag flying over the Capitol was lowered and replaced by "the Union Flag of the American states." Thomas Nelson hurried off to Philadelphia with copies of the resolves, and Pendleton sent other copies to the other colonies to encourage similar action.

The next day Williamsburg celebrated the unanimous vote with a parade in Waller's Grove, behind the Capitol. The text of the resolves was read aloud. Patriotic toasts—to the American independent states, to the Grand Congress of the United States and their respective legislatures, to General Washington and victory to the American arms—were punctuated with salutes from artillery and small arms. The soldiers "partook of the refreshments prepared for them by the affection of their countrymen, and the evening concluded with illuminations, and other demonstrations of joy."

Also on May 15 the Virginia Convention acted on Pendleton's second resolution, "That a committee be appointed to prepare a DECLARATION OF RIGHTS, and such a plan of government as will be most likely to maintain peace and order in this colony, and secure substantial and equal liberty to the people." Archibald Cary was chairman of the committee of thirty-odd members chosen to draft the two documents. They could find no precedent for a formal statement of the principles on which government ought to rest or for a written constitution based on the separation of executive, legislative, and judicial powers; but everyone in public life had ideas about what was needed. The rights of American colonies had been listed many times in the past ten years, and the behavior of crown officials everywhere had provoked criticism and ideas about practical ways to control them. Cary's committee, therefore, was troubled with too many ideas and too little agreement.

First they worked on the text of the declaration of rights, which would lay a philosophical foundation for the constitution and perhaps serve as a preamble to it. In the opinion of one of the members, Edmund Randolph, the "many projects" proposed revealed "ardor for political notice" rather than "ripeness in political wisdom." When George Mason arrived, late, he was added to the committee, and his proposals quickly "swallowed up all the rest by fixing the grounds and plan, which after great discussion and correction were finally ratified."

The extent of Henry's participation in the discussions was not recorded, but Randolph credited him with the fifteenth and sixteenth rights—frequent recurrence to fundamental principles, and the free exercise of religion. Mason was the undisputed author of the first fourteen articles. The entire text was argued and somewhat amended in committee and then approved by the convention on June 12. Posterity still regards the Virginia Declaration of Rights as a noble document, and it is still a model for new nations setting up democratic governments.

Work on the text of the constitution continued until the end of June, interrupted by more immediate problems of preparedness and defense against Dunmore's activities and of supplies and men for the Continental Army. Though President Pendleton was too busy with emergencies to attend committee meetings regularly, he kept in close touch with their work. Late in May he informed Jefferson: "The Political Cooks are busy in preparing the dish," but he expects the session to be a long one; "indeed the importance of our business requires it and we must sweat it out with Fortitude."

Generally satisfied with familiar local government and election procedures, the committee needed to replace crown appointees with elected officials in a pattern that would maintain a balanced division of power at the state level. They hoped to achieve the balance by limiting the executive, by preserving the bicameral legislature and removing from the upper house all executive and judicial functions. Though these constitution-makers agreed on broad objectives, many of them were lawyers and political philosophers, either professional or amateur, who vigorously debated the character of each part of the machine they were designing and argued with gusto about how the parts should be assembled for efficient performance.

These differences of sentiment Henry labeled "democratic" and "aristocratic." He found his own plans for a "democratic" form of government "precisely" outlined in his friend John Adams's pamphlet, *Thoughts on Government*, which the author sent him. Adams proposed a lower house elected by the people annually; a smaller upper house elected annually by the lower; a governor chosen annually by the two houses together but with a veto on legislation; judges and military officers appointed by the governor with the advice of the upper house or by the legislature. Adams assured Henry privately that he should not hesitate to use every means to propel a democratic constitution through the convention, since no one was "so competent to the task as the author of the first Virginia resolutions against the Stamp Act, who will have the glory with posterity of beginning and concluding this great revolution."

Another pamphlet from Philadelphia was being studied by the

"aristocratic" members of the committee. Braxton had sent down a plan prepared by an anonymous "Virginian," in Henry's view "a silly thing" recommending a three-year term for the lower house, popularly elected; an upper house and a governor chosen for life by the lower house; civil, judicial, and military officers appointed by the governor.

On Monday, June 24, Cary presented the committee's draft. After three days of discussion and amendment in the Committee of the Whole, the convention on June 29 unanimously adopted "The Constitution, or Form of Government, agreed to and resolved upon by the Delegates and Representatives of the several counties and corporations of Virginia." The new machine was as "democratic" as Henry could have wished, if not so well balanced. In the state's General Assembly, the House of Delegates was elected annually and given power to originate all legislation. The colonial councilors were replaced by twenty-four senators, elected for four-year terms and given only legislative functions. The governor, chosen annually by joint ballot of the Senate and House of Delegates, could serve no more than three successive terms, and he then became ineligible for four years. He had no veto, no power to make appointments above the county level, and he could take executive action only with the advice and consent of a Council of State, composed of eight members chosen like the governor but for three-year terms.

These limitations, in Henry's opinion, made the executive "a dependent instead of a coordinate power." In committee he exerted the full strength of his eloquence and influence in favor of an executive veto. He "exhausted the topic" and bombarded his colleagues with references to the theories of Montesquieu and other philosophers. Yet he lost a theoretical point which would become one of great practical importance to him when, on June 29, the convention acted on Article XXII and introduced the new government by casting their ballots for governor. Out of 106 votes, Henry received sixty, and the convention formally declared him to be "the governor of the commonwealth of Virginia."

On the day that he took the oath of office, July 5, Purdie's *Virginia Gazette* published one of the most heart-warming of the many congratulations he received—an address of the First and Second Virginia Regiments:

Permit us, with the sincerest sentiments of respect and joy, to congratulate your Excellency upon your unsolicited promotion to the highest honours a grateful people can bestow.

Uninfluenced by private ambition, regardless of sordid interest, you have uniformly pursued the general good of your country; and have taught the world, that an ingenuous love of the rights of mankind, an inflexible resolution, and a steady perseverance in the practice of every private and publick virtue, lead directly to preferment, and give the best title to the honours of an uncorrupted and vigorous state.

Once happy under your military command, we hope for more extensive blessings from your civil administration. . . . [We are] happy that we have lived to see the day when freedom and equal right, established by the voice of the people, shall prevail through the land.

V.

Citizen of the Commonwealth, 1776-1799

THE day that Governor Henry took the oath of office, the lieutenant governor, John Page, was alarmed about his health. He informed their friend Jefferson that Henry was "very ill" and speculated about what might happen "if he should die." The disease was apparently malaria; while its cause was then unknown, experience showed that quinine in the form of "Peruvian bark" relieved the ague or "chills and fever" so common in the tidewater and piedmont. Henry's malaria was probably the debilitating kind now considered one of the worst of tropical diseases, and it recurred from time to time for the remainder of his life. When attacks came, he attributed the feeling of fatigue partly to overwork and tried to rest, in bed if possible. During the first year of his governorship he retired to Scotchtown for about five weeks in the summer and two weeks in the fall.

When he was resident in the Governor's Palace, his hostess was his sister Anne Christian, who came to Williamsburg with her husband in 1775 when he was lieutenant colonel of the First Virginia Regiment. In the fall of 1777 Henry's second wife Dorothea, daughter of his old friend Nathaniel West Dandridge, replaced Anne Christian as hostess, and Henry's younger children joined them. The family maintained a simple style of living but with some of the elegance Dorothea was accustomed to, and they met the social demands of his office with simple dignity. One child was born here August 2, 1778, Dorothea's first, a daughter named for her, Dorothea Spotswood Henry.

During the war years the new machinery of state worked smoothly enough. John Page and the Council of State acted with the governor when he was present, without him when he was absent. The Speaker of the House of Delegates—first Pendleton, then Wythe, then Harrison—held the position of greatest power in the commonwealth, but everyone was too busy with the immediate problems of wartime emergencies to find time for power politics.

In July Dunmore's raids continued in the Potomac; then he left Hampton Roads in August. During the summer Great Britain was increasing her war effort. General Sir William Howe arrived in New York in September. When he moved south in December, there was panic in Philadelphia and Virginia was threatened. Henry stepped up aid to Washington and sent him two Virginia regiments. At the same time militia recruitment was increased to provide defense of the frontiers, against the Cherokee in the southwest and British-Indian activity in the northwest. The endless negotiations for purchases of arms, food, blankets, and other supplies extended to the West Indies and Europe.

With so many scarcities, there was some disagreement about priorities. Henry's critics, including St. George Tucker, thought he sent too many men and supplies to the north, and in 1777 and 1778 also to the Carolinas, leaving Virginia's resources too depleted for safety in case of attack. Financial problems were aggravated by the staggering rate of inflation and by speculation in war materials and food supplies.

Among the few bright spots were Washington's victories at Trenton and Princeton. Then came Burgoyne's surrender at Saratoga and the treaty of alliance with France. In Williamsburg the surrender was celebrated with a "feu de joy"—military parade, artillery salutes, and a military review on Market Square. A gill of rum was issued to each soldier "in evidence of the Governor's hearty congratulation" on the occasion, which closed with the ringing of bells and illuminations. Governor and Council of State also ordered a day of Thanksgiving in all Virginia churches and congregations of Christians.

The greatest achievement on Henry's gubernatorial record was George Rogers Clark's conquest of the northwest. While Henry was ill at Scotchtown in August 1776 Clark called on him requesting powder for the protection of Kentucky settlements against Indian and British raids. With the governor's letter of approval, Clark went on to Williamsburg and got powder from the Council of Sate. In December 1777, after a harrowing year in the Kentucky settlements, Clark returned to Williamsburg and proposed an expedition into the Illinois country against Kaskaskia, the center of British organization of Indian raids in Kentucky. With the approval of Jefferson, Mason, and Wythe, the House of Delegates joined Governor and Council in a secret order to Clark, who captured Kaskaskia July 4, 1778. In December the General Assembly created the vast new county of Illinois.

Just before Henry retired from office, war suddenly came to Virginia in May 1779, when an amphibious expedition under General Edward Mathew and Commodore Sir George Collier took Portsmouth and burned Suffolk, destroying ships and supplies valued at two million pounds. After two weeks the British forces withdrew, before effective resistance could be mobilized.

Governor Henry had no time for constructive reforms. This work was being done in the House of Delegates, where Jefferson and Wythe returned from the Continental Congress to do it; for they considered the reorganization of the courts and revision of the laws the most important part of the revolution.

On June 1, 1779, Jefferson succeeded him as governor and Henry retired to Leatherwood, a ten-thousand-acre farm in Henry County, about 180 miles southwest of Richmond. Leatherwood Creek, a tributary of the Dan River, flowed along the foothills of the Blue Ridge, through the beautiful country William Byrd called "the Land of Eden," where Henry hoped the bracing climate might restore his health. The year before, he had sold Scotchtown for £5,000—a handsome profit, even in depreciated currency—and bought the big frontier tract partly as an investment, partly as a refuge from the danger of enemy action.

His retirement lasted less than a year. In May 1780 the new delegate from Henry County made the six-day journey to Richmond, the new capital. He immediately took his place as leader of the House of Delegates and occupied it until 1784, when he was again chosen governor. After two terms, he declined to serve a third and again retired to a new home, this one in Prince Edward County near Hampden-Sydney College. He planned to resume the practice of law in order to support his still-growing family. Fayette Henry, born in October 1785, was Dorothea's fifth child, and her eleventh would arrive before Henry's death.

Though he refused appointment as a delegate to the Constitutional Convention of 1787, Henry interrupted his law practice to represent Prince Edward County in the fall session of the General Assembly and again in the Virginia Constitutional Convention of June 1788.

In the early years of the Commonwealth, politics was still personal, for political parties would not appear until the late 1790's. Everyone in public life was by definition "republican." Whether a man might wear today's label of "liberal" or "conservative" depended upon his attitude toward the timing of a specific proposal or the methods to be used in putting a program into action. Though Henry, "the great liberal," often took a conservative position, he was in reality more consistent on broad issues than many of his critics. Today when he is labeled spokesman for "the common man," he is criticized because he had no broad program for legal and social reforms. In fact he was a practical man, not a philosopher, and he represented the practical interests of the voters who sent him to legislative bodies. He was no theorist, like Jefferson and Madison, and he distrusted innovative, theoretical programs. He was sincere when he declared that he had "but one lamp" by which his feet were guided, "the lamp of experience."

Nor did he ride with the tide of public opinion. He maintained control of Virginia in the 1780's in spite of occasional advocacy of unpopular measures. For example, he defended Baptist preachers before the revolution in their fight for freedom of worship; yet he opposed Jefferson's Statute for Religous Freedom when Madison sponsored it in the House of Delegates because he thought it went too far in permitting the choice of no religion at all—atheism. A sincerely religious man himself, growing more so with advancing age, he preferred a law that would provide tax support for churches of all denominations.

He understood the weaknesses of the Continental Congress as clearly as anyone else and urged the strengthening of the Confederation, particularly in the regulation of commerce. But in 1786 he was alarmed when a proposed treaty with Spain offered to surrender the navigation of the Mississippi for twenty-five years in return for special commercial privileges in Spanish ports. A consistent spokesman for the frontier, he saw this threat to western interests as a northern combination of seven commercial states against the interests of six southern states. Now distrusting the seven-state majority, he opposed the "consolidated" government under the Constitution on the principle of states' rights and attended the Richmond Convention of 1788 to prevent its adoption in Virginia.

When the convention met in June, Madison expected to get a fifty-vote majority in favor of adoption, for he numbered among his supporters Pendleton, Wythe, Marshall, Edmund Randolph, and the attorney general, Col. James Innes, second only to Henry in eloquence. Henry spoke on eighteen days of the twenty-three, as often as eight times a day, and as long as seven hours at a time. This convention had a shorthand reporter, David Robertson, who prepared abstracts of the speeches. Of the 600-odd pages of his printed report, Henry's speeches occupy about forty. What a tour de force! St. George Tucker, who was present in Madison's camp, described the performance:

> The variety of arguments, which Mr. Henry generally presented in his speeches, addressed to the capacities, prejudices, and individual interests of his hearers, made his speeches very unequal. . . . If he soared at times, like the eagle, and seemed like the bird of Jove to be armed with thunder, he did not disdain to stoop like the hawk to seize his prey—but the instant that he had done it, rose in pursuit of another quarry.

Henry examined the Constitution, article by article, and found in every department too much federal power at the expense of the sovereign rights of the states and the human rights and privileges of the citizens. The Constitution, he feared, would "destroy the state governments, and swallow the liberties of the people, without previous notice." He was especially suspicious of the implied powers. "We are giving power," he declared, "they are getting power; judge, then, on which side the implication will be used." In his opinion, "all the good qualities of this government are founded" on "a supposition" that all federal officials would be "honest," while the "defective and imperfect" Constitution "puts it in their power to perpetuate the worst of mischiefs, should they be bad men."

Again and again he returned to the need for a federal bill of rights similar to Virginia's. He hoped to postpone the vote for adoption until a bill of rights could be added. But the vote on June 25, eighty-nine to seventy-nine, was for immediate adoption with a recommendation that a bill of rights be added as amendments.

To ensure the election of senators who would press for the amendments, in October Henry returned to the General Assembly, where the first federal senators would be chosen. Washington, at Mount Vernon, anxiously awaiting news of the outcome, found the early "Accounts from Richmond . . . very impropitious." He informed Madison: "The Whole proceedings of the Assembly, *it is said* may be summed up in one word, to wit, that the Edicts of Mr. H---- are enregistered with less opposition by the majority of that body, than those of the Grand Monarch are in the Parliaments of France. He has only to say let this be Law, and it is Law." Henry himself refused to run, on the plea of ill health, but he managed the defeat of Madison and the choice of two antifederalists, Richard Henry Lee and William Grayson. Jefferson, hoping for the election of Madison, grumbled: "Mr. Henry is omnipotent in Virginia."

Until November 1791 Henry continued to represent Prince Edward County in the House of Delegates, though with frequent leaves of absence. Even after he declined reelection in 1792 and finally retired from political office, friends continued to consult him, and he remained the dominant figure in Virginia politics. As Irving Brant complains in his biography of Madison, "Whatever was attempted, in the perfection of infant republican institutions, the first question had to be: Will Patrick Henry oppose it? And the query as to action usually was: How can we slip it past him?"

When political parties developed in national politics, both Federalists and Republicans tried to woo Henry out of retirement. Washington offered him a cabinet post as secretary of state, an appointment as chief justice, and diplomatic missions to Spain and France. In spite of his warm admiration for the president, he declined all federal office.

Jefferson and Madison hoped that the strong states' rights plank in the Republican platform would persuade him to bring Virginia into the Republican camp. In foreign affairs their pro-French attitude was expected to appeal to his gratitude for French aid in the American Revolution and his outspoken sympathy with the early aims of the French Revolution. But after 1793, when King Louis XVI was executed and Lafayette imprisoned, Henry saw in the place of our old ally a bloody despotism paying homage to a Goddess of Reason, and he could no longer support Republican foreign policy.

His final break with the Republicans came in 1799 over an application of states' rights. The year before, Jefferson and Madison had responded to the Federalist Alien and Sedition Acts with the Kentucky and Virginia Resolutions, in which the two state legislatures declared these acts of Congress unconstitutional, "void, and of no force." While neither resolution proposed specific state action to nullify the Alien and Sedition laws, two possibilities were obvious—either civil disobedience or secession. Washington, in retirement at Mount Vernon, alarmed at this Republican threat to the union, asked Henry to stand for election to the House of Delegates, where he would be able to counteract Republican influence. Henry, too, thought the situation critical and agreed to appear at Charlotte Courthouse in March and deliver a Federalist message.

He argued that the resolutions were unconstitutional because only the Supreme Court could nullify an act of Congress; that civil disobedience would provoke civil war because federal law would be enforced by military power, if necessary; that secession would be reckless and premature because peaceful means of redress of grievances were available and should be tried first. In brief, this was no time for another revolution, and he advised that government under the Constitution be given an opportunity to work out sectional differences by constitutional procedures.

The other speaker that day, John Randolph of Roanoke, was entering politics as a Republican candidate for the House of Representatives. Thus it happened that the two most eloquent orators in Virginia history appeared together, Henry speaking for the last time, Randolph for the first, and both were elected. Henry's election did not affect Republican control of the General Assembly because he died before the autumn meeting of the legislature. But his appearance at Charlotte Courthouse produced strong reactions among party politicians and seriously affected his reputation in history. Federalists, acclaiming his courage and patriotism, called it the noblest act of his career. Republicans saw it as a repudiation of the principles of a lifetime; Jefferson called him "the Great Apostate." In contrast, Henry kept his temper even during the vicious party warfare. His harshest criticism was directed toward Republican admiration of everything French, the pretentiousness of Jefferson's French chef, menus, and wines—he did not approve of gentlemen's "abjuring their native victuals."

After he retired from public office, Henry was busy with private affairs. He had served Virginia almost thirty years, his political ambitions were well satisfied, and he did not want to suffer the fate of most revolutionary leaders—bankruptcy from too much time spent in public office and the consequent neglect of personal business. He explained to his daughter Elizabeth in 1791: "I am obliged to be very industrious and to take on me great Fatigue to clear myself of Debt. I hope to be able to accomplish this in a year or two if it pleases God to continue me in Health and Strength."

Instead of a year or two, he spent four years making money in land speculation, farming, and law practice. When he retired from private business in 1794, he had cleared himself of debt and accumulated an estate that would keep his family in easy circumstances and provide for the education of the younger children. He now owned three prosperous farms on the Staunton River near Charlotte Courthouse—Long Island, Seven Islands, and the Red Hill plantation that would be his last residence.

The volume of his law business was as great in the commonwealth as it had been in the colony, and his prestige now gave him important civil and criminal cases with correspondingly large fees. His most important civil case, *Jones v. Walker,* opened in November 1791 in the United States District Court at Richmond. William Jones, British merchant, brought suit against Dr. Thomas Walker to collect an old debt dated 1772. Under the terms of the treaty of peace in 1783, pre-revolutionary debts could be recovered in the federal courts, and the Constitution recognized these terms of the treaty.

However, the sovereign state of Virginia in a law of October 1777 permitted money due to British creditors to be paid into the state treasury, and with inflated currency. Virginians who had taken advantage of this opportunity were unwilling to pay the debts a second time, and the suit of *Jones v. Walker* was a test case. The district judge and two Supreme Court justices heard the case. Jones employed four able lawyers, and Henry's associates were John Marshall, James Innes, and Alexander Campbell. For once in his life Henry's critics agreed that his argument was carefully prepared and demonstrated a surprising mastery of international law. He was addressing learned jurists, and for emotional appeal he drew upon the history of the American Revolution. The judges reserved their decision, and the case was continued to May 1793. As in 1763 in Hanover, so in 1793 in Richmond the judges decided for the plaintiff and a jury was chosen to determine the amount to be paid. This jury, however, disagreed, and British creditors later collected, if at all, from federal funds.

In criminal cases tried before county juries "the great Patrick" used his dramatic talents to such effect that much of the folklore associated with his name in the Southside dates from this practice. He played a starring role in early Virginia's most notorious murder case. In April 1793 Richard Randolph, elder brother of John Randolph of Roanoke and stepson of Judge St. George Tucker, was tried in Cumberland County Court on a charge of infanticide. Marshall and Campbell were preparing Randolph's defense when Henry was offered 500 guineas to assist them in the courtroom. Much of the evidence was circumstantial and inconclusive; some of it was based on gossip. Under Henry's skillful examination several key witnesses exposed their prejudices, and their testimony was made to appear untrustworthy—and even ridiculous. The jury decided that the charge was supported by insufficient evidence, and Randolph was released.

Henry's declining years were spent in his "Garden Spot of Virginia." The simple house at Red Hill was crowded with young children and grandchildren, his "companions and friends." Still "abounding in good humor," the old man often entertained them with his fiddle, playing improvised tunes to suit their games and moods. He could still pitch his magnificent voice with the old skill: standing beside the house, he called instructions to servants at work in the rich bottomlands half-a-mile away.

He spent many hours with favorite books, notably the Bible, and his conversation grew more religious and didactic. He could quote for a grandson the simple moral code learned from his Uncle Patrick, knowing that he had followed it faithfully all his life: "To be true and just in all my dealings. To bear no malice nor hatred in my heart. To keep my hands from picking and stealing. Not to covet other men's goods; but to learn and labor truly to get my own living, and to do my duty in that state of life unto which it shall please God to call me."

Patrick Henry died June 6, 1799, surrounded by his immediate family. His plain, flat tombstone in the garden at Red Hill carries a simple inscription: "His fame his best epitaph."

A Bibliographical Note

William Wirt, in his *Sketches of the Life and Character of Patrick Henry* (Philadelphia, 1817, and many later editions), used relatively few criticisms of his hero. The correspondence is now widely scattered, but one series of letters has been printed: *The Confidential Letters from Thomas Jefferson to William Wirt. Being Reminiscences of Patrick Henry* (Philadelphia, 1912).

Moses Coit Tyler, *Patrick Henry* (Boston and New York, 1887) is a scholarly, well balanced account of Henry's life until the last decade, when the interpretation takes on a strong Jeffersonian bias.

William Wirt Henry, for his *Patrick Henry: Life, Correspondence and Speeches* (3 vols., New York, 1891), collected his grandfather's surviving papers, family letters and traditions, Wirt's correspondence, and anecdotes from Southside Virginia folklore.

George Morgan, *The True Patrick Henry* (Philadelphia and London, 1907) is readable rather than scholarly. Morgan used public records, newspapers, and William Wirt Henry's materials preserved at Red Hill to portray Henry as an interesting human being. Since Morgan saw the Red Hill collection in 1906, it has been dispersed; many of the papers sold at auction in 1910 were purchased by autograph collectors.

Bernard Mayo, "The Enigma of Patrick Henry," in *Myths and Men* (Athens, Georgia, 1957), 1-23, examined the myths and contradictions surrounding the historical character and used light and dark images to make a three-dimensional picture of the man.

Robert D. Meade, *Patrick Henry* (2 vols., Philadelphia and New York, 1957, 1969) is the most recent and detailed biography. The bibliography and footnotes are valuable for the present location of Henry's papers and of comments about him.